PA$$ING ON

Gather yourselves together, and hear, ye sons of Jacob:
and hearken unto Israel your father.

Genesis 49:1

PA$$ING ON

WHAT'S FAIR IN FAMILY INHERITANCE?

Ruth Dixon-Mueller

Afterword by
Frederick Hertz, Attorney

ISBN-13: 9781546991472
ISBN-10: 1546991476

CONTENTS

INTRODUCTION

Everyone has an inheritance story to tell.

It might be a story of no bequest at all. "You're writing about inheritance? Ha! My parents had nothing. I left home at sixteen to go to work, and that was it. The whole concept is a strange one to me."

It might be a story of families gone wrong. "My mother left everything to me. She never forgave my sister for getting pregnant and then marrying who she did. I shared my inheritance with her so we and the kids could all be family."

It could be a story of regret. "I wish Dad had talked to us before he left everything to his wife. She's executor too. Now she has things that belonged to our mother, and she gets to live in the house for the rest of her life. We could die before she does!"

Or a story of frustration with the tangled affairs of a loved one who died without leaving a will. Of secretive executors, promises not kept ("that clock should have gone to *me!*"), unanticipated debts. The scenarios are many; the emotions palpable. "It isn't fair!"

If we're in our fifties or sixties or beyond and have accumulated a few things (or far more than a few), we're probably making our wills and estate plans. Perhaps we prepared them long ago and it's time to take another look. Perhaps we have no spouse or kids and don't think it's important. But it is. Every one of us who is over fifty—and younger, too, if we have assets and/or dependents—needs to make plans for what will happen to our property, our personal belongings and our bodies when we die.

The over-fifties comprise two generations. The *oldest*, born during the Great Depression or the Second World War, are now in their seventies or eighties on up. Ready or not, they (we) are on the front lines of our own mortality, which means that making or updating our estate plans is a matter of urgency. The *middle* generation of postwar Baby Boomers are now in their fifties or sixties. Adult children of aging or deceased parents, most are also parents and even grandparents themselves. Labeled the Sandwich Generation because of their obligations to both older and younger generations, they are also called the Threshold Generation because they are on the verge of (or passing) retirement age.[1] Members of this middle generation may yet receive an inheritance from their parents even as they decide—at least for now—who their own beneficiaries will be.

Among Americans aged sixty-five and older, two-thirds say they have written a will.[2] What happens if we die without one? Dying *intestate* (that is, lacking a "testament") means that we waive our right to decide. Perhaps that doesn't matter to us. But by not making a will— or by postponing until it's too late—we are in fact taking a position, not avoiding one. We are choosing one option over another. Probate courts in every state rely on statutory rules of descent and distribution for allocating the assets of someone who dies intestate to his or her next of kin (or not-so-next, if close links cannot be traced). These intestacy rules may reflect what we might decide on our own, or they may not. Can they be challenged by the living? Almost never.

This is not a book about how to write a will or prepare an estate plan, however. The American Bar Association's *Guide to Wills and Estates* claims to contain *Everything You Need to Know about Wills, Estates, Trusts, and Taxes.* Or consider Nolo's *Plan Your Estate: All You Need to Know About Wills & Trusts, Estate & Gift Taxes, Avoiding Probate, Powers of Attorney & Living Wills* by attorney Denis Clifford. These and other manuals offer comprehensive advice from the legal point of view, although all advise us to consult an attorney. They cannot address the peculiarities of our own situations, however, nor anticipate how each of us considers questions of what's fair and what's not from our personal points of view.

Passing On is a book about death (yes, *our* death) and about ideas of fairness and justice in family inheritance writ large and small. It considers some of the many dilemmas we face as testators—that is, as makers of a Last Will and Testament—when we choose what to pass on to our survivors and who to appoint as our personal representatives to carry out our wishes when we die. Are we being fair in the decisions we make? (What will our survivors think?) Most of us have also inherited something, or will do so in the future, at the death of a grandparent, parent, spouse, or other relative. Were they fair in the decisions *they* made? (What do *we* think?) Moreover, we are all members of a society in which inherited wealth reinforces the social and economic inequalities among us. Is *inheritance itself* fair? (What does everyone think?)

P art One of this book views family inheritance from the perspective of social justice and the inequalities among us. Chapter One begins with the story of an idea that seems unremarkable to us today: the idea that each one of us is free to decide who will inherit our worldly goods when we die. Although the concept of *testamentary freedom* has ancient origins, its historical path through English common law to the United States and a handful of other common law countries is a relatively narrow one. In most parts of our contemporary world, civil codes or religious laws or custom dictates who among the surviving kin or community receives the property, and perhaps the status or title, of the deceased. In contrast, we are free to make these moral choices on our own. How do we do this? What choices do we make?

Chapter Two explores the philosophical background of current debates about economic inequalities and individual opportunities in American society. The intergenerational transmission of wealth and its associated privileges serves as a flashpoint for contrasting ideological positions about individual freedoms and the role of the family, on the one hand, and social justice and the role of the state, on the other. How do we balance our notions of what's fair in our own families with what's fair in our communities and society at large?

Chapter Three, which describes inheritance patterns in the United States today, contains a specific message: economic inequalities and uncertainties abound. They have a time dimension as well, one that is associated in part with how long we expect to live. How does the overall rise in female and male life expectancies affect the timing of bequests from the oldest to the middle generation? Given these trends, is the predominant pattern of leaving everything to a surviving spouse fair to the offspring? What about gifts to other beneficiaries? And what about contributions to organizations and institutions that promote the common good? Who gives and who doesn't? What do we make of these practices?

Part Two lays out an array of arguments about what's fair and what's not as viewed from different perspectives within the family. Chapter

Four focuses on the parent who, in making or revising a will, must decide how to allocate shares of his or her estate to adult children who may have quite different needs or "deserts"—and possibly to stepchildren or grandchildren as well. Chapter Five focuses on adult siblings who, in turn, must decide how to divide up personal property that has been left to them collectively. Finally, given the many legitimate (and some not so legitimate) claims of what's fair both in principle and in practice, Chapter Six asks whether fairness can be negotiated among family members as part of a participatory process of making or revising an estate plan. Initiating informal conversations or more formal mediated sessions with family members can provide important insights into their hopes and concerns as well as our own. It can also help to create a sense among survivors that the decision-making process was a fair one and that everyone at least had a chance to be heard.

Wills are uncanny and electric documents," writes Janet Malcolm in her book about Alice B. Toklas and Gertrude Stein, *Two Lives*. "They lie dormant for years, and then spring to life when their author dies, as if death were rain. Their effect on those they enrich or disappoint is never negligible, and sometimes unexpectedly charged."[3]

At her death in France in 1947, Stein left her money and collection of paintings and writings to Alice, her intimate partner of forty years, the proceeds of which were to support Toklas for "her useful life." But the final trust destination of these treasures was Stein's nephew Allan. "Stein disliked Allan," writes Malcolm, "but still felt compelled to make him her heir." And so the story goes: Allan dies; Alice is tricked out of the estate by a trustee in collusion with Allan's adult children; Alice dies in poverty at age 89. What's fair about that?

Wills, says Malcolm, "are not written in stone—for all their granite legal language—and they can be bent to subvert the wishes of the writer." So, too, can the writer of the will be swayed by guilt-inducing norms that favor or even compel the naming of kin (no matter how distant) as "the natural objects of our bounty" over other beneficiaries (no matter how close) when passing on our worldly goods.

For the will maker and for the estate planning professional alike, the goal of *Passing On* is to raise questions and challenge assumptions about what's fair and what's not in family inheritance. The book is intended to engage our social conscience by posing multiple and often competing points of view about what we choose to leave to family members (however we define "family"), to persons outside the family, and to organizations whose work we support.

Our testamentary freedom allows us to make personal moral choices about the legacy we leave behind. Engaging with the ideas about fairness and justice in this book may help us to make the "right" decisions, whatever they may be. It may confirm the choices we've already made. Or it might even change our minds.

PART ONE

SOCIAL INEQUALITIES

CHAPTER ONE

TESTAMENTARY FREEDOM: THE EVOLUTION OF AN IDEA

At the time when you end the days of your life, in the hour of death, distribute your inheritance. *Joshua ben Sirach, second century BCE*

There was a time when we might have pronounced our final testament rather grandly (or feebly) from our deathbed, surrounded by distraught family members, wide-eyed children, faithful servants, the local priest and a hound or spaniel or two.

These days, we are urged to distribute our worldly goods through our Last Will and Testament while we are still of sound mind, long before the end is near. In matters of inheritance we have moved from the deathbed to the lawyer's office, the spiritual to the practical, the moral to the legalistic, and the spoken to the written (now printed or digital) word. But there is continuity as well: the words, derived from the ancients, still stand.

Testament. In its mundane definition, a testament (Latin *testamentum*) is "a proof of something" and also "a person's will, especially the part relating to personal property." It has a religious connotation of witnessing as well, as we know from the Old and New Testaments. And so it is that today that we have a *testator*—the maker of a will—together with witnesses who testify to its authenticity and to the mental capacities of the maker. And so it is, too, that we die *testate* or *intestate*, depending on whether or not we have performed the legal ritual.

> Everyone who dies leaves something behind. Everyone who owns property leaves it behind. But to whom does this property belong? [4]

Americans since colonial times have enjoyed the freedom to dispose of their real and personal property upon their death as they see fit. Indeed, in composing our personal wills we are a little like benevolent (or not so benevolent) dictators. We may give everything to charity or to a friend or caregiver and nothing to our children. We may endow our offspring equally or indulge a favored daughter and disown an errant son. We may change our minds and the terms of our will, break promises, reward and punish family members (even a spouse) and, in general, behave well or badly, as we wish.

Freedom of bequest may seem natural and fair to us today. But it's not that way to everyone. Indeed, the American parents' ability to disinherit their children if they decide to do so is "unimaginable to most people of the world".[5] In almost all European and South American countries and in jurisdictions of Islamic law, children (and spouses) receive a predetermined portion of the deceased person's estate based solely on the fact of their relationship. They cannot be disinherited, no matter what the will may say.

Our legal system does offer some protections for dependent family members, however. In the more than forty states with common law jurisdictions, a spouse or child can appeal to the probate courts for a portion of the estate if the will does not adequately provide for them.[6] In community property states, surviving spouses automatically retain the half share of the marital property that is already theirs by right, as well as any separate property they might own.

Potential heirs have other legal tools for challenging a will. They may claim that the document is fraudulent, for instance, or that the deceased was mentally incompetent at the time of its writing or was under the influence of a greedy manipulator.[7]

A will can also be contested on technical grounds. A probate judge could rule it invalid because of an incorrect signature, say, or illegible handwriting (if it is a holographic will), improper filing, or some other fault. Perhaps the witnesses were not aware that the document being signed was a will. Law professor Melanie Leslie writes that judicial insistence on strict compliance with even "trifling legal formalities" can sometimes render the document—and thus the expressed wishes of the deceased—null and void, no matter how reasonable they may be.[8]

In essence, however, our laws grant testators the final say. As a Pennsylvania judge once explained to a presumably unhappy plaintiff in the "Gerard Will Case,"

> Respected men and women, as well as eccentric people, sometimes make sound and sometimes eccentric wills.... While it is difficult for many people to understand how or why a man is permitted to make a strange or unusual bequest, especially if he has children or close relatives living, we must remember that under the law of Pennsylvania, a man's prejudices are a part of his liberty. He has a right to the control of his property while living, and may bestow it as he sees fit at his death.[9]

Where did the radical idea of testamentary freedom come from? It was not new to the American colonies. Rather, the practice of writing a Last Will and Testament migrated to America with the early settlers as part of English Common law.[10] The English, in turn, inherited the practice from the Romans during their four-century occupation of Britain following the invasion of 54 BCE. But the Romans came up with the idea long before that.

More than twenty-five hundred years ago, a body of Roman civil, criminal and religious law called the *Twelve Tables* (451 to 449 BCE) set forth the rules of succession that would apply "if anyone who has no direct heir dies intestate."[11] The word *intestate* rings loud and clear: that the law made provisions for this eventuality means that the *testament* must have already been a common practice by then.

And so it was. In his classic book *Ancient Law* (1856), English historian Henry Sumner Maine describes the scene. Imagine a Patrician Assembly of high-ranking citizens in the Roman Republic. In the presence of witnesses, the aging patriarch of a great household (a *paterfamilias*) proclaims the transfer to his designated heirs of his landed estates, homes and personal property along with his ceremonial rights and obligations, his position in the community, and all of the people under his guardianship including multiple generations of family members, sundry household followers and slaves.

As the centuries passed, written wills replaced living oral testaments and plebeians (common citizens) adopted the practice in their own assemblies. But the ritual remained: male citizens presented their wills to the assembly in front of witnesses, whereupon the documents were sealed and stored in religious sites to be opened after the testator's death.

Why were personal wills so important? In the early days of the Republic they most likely filled a gap in how property, power and privilege were to be passed down through the generations. But the posting of the Twelve Tables and their intestacy rules added new urgency to the practice. According to Maine, patricians lived "in horror of intestacy" and were determined to avoid it.

The intestacy rules were these: the estate of a man who died without a will passed first to his direct descendants, if he had any. If not, his people and property passed to his "nearest agnate," that is, to a descendant in the male bloodline from a common male progenitor. (The children of a brother or uncle could inherit, for example, but not those of a sister or aunt.) Wives did not inherit in intestate cases nor, it appears, did daughters, all of whom fell under the guardianship of a designated male relative.[12] But the Twelve Tables excluded another class of potential heirs as well: grown sons who had been legally emancipated from the authority of their fathers. Once they were legally free, the law considered them "strangers to the rights of kinship and aliens from the blood."[13] Maine contends that the ancient Romans cherished their testamentary freedom not so much "as a means of *disinheriting* a Family, or of effecting the unequal distribution of patrimony." Rather, he claims, they valued their freedom "for the assistance it gave in *making provision for* a Family, and in dividing the inheritance more evenly and fairly than the Law of Intestate Succession would have divided it."[14]

"But what was the Family?" Maine asks. "The [Roman] Law defined it one way—natural affection another."[15] This duality confronts us today. The intestacy rules of succession in the state in which we live (and die) may or may not correspond with our "natural affections" or our sense of fairness and responsibility. And if they do not, then making a will can put things right, at least from our singular point of view.

The idea of testamentary freedom journeyed from ancient Rome to the American colonies through more than sixteen centuries of English history. Not surprisingly, it experienced a number of jolts and displacements along the way.

The first was the collapse of the Western Roman Empire in the fifth century. As the occupiers withdrew from England, Roman jurisprudence faded and local populations turned to Anglo Saxon forms of governance, property arrangements and inheritance.

The second seismic jolt occurred five hundred years later with the Norman invasion of 1066. The occupiers this time imposed the French feudal system with its rule of absolute monarchs over all of the kingdom's land, wealth and its people.

Five hundred years after *that*, during the reign of Henry VIII in 1540, a restive English Parliament enacted a Statute of Wills that restored to a landowner, or "freeholder," the power to devise by will the greater part of his real property to whomever he chose.[16] If a man died without a will, the intestate rules of succession would apply. These rules were remarkably similar to the Roman Twelve Tables, with one important exception: real property was to pass to the *oldest surviving son of the deceased* (or to a grandson if no son survived), following the Norman custom of primogeniture.

The Statute of Wills did not apply to movable property, however, which was handled by the ecclesiastical courts until absolute testamentary freedom became the general principle of English law in 1724.[17] But the Statute was remarkably liberal in its pronouncement that a landholder could bequeath his real property "...for the advancement of his wife, preferment of his children, and payment of his debts or otherwise at his will and pleasure; *any law, statute, custom or other things to the contrary notwithstanding.*"[18]

Did this mean that women had the same rights to inherit and bequeath real property that men did? No. Although wives and daughters could inherit, married women under English Common law lived in the shadows of their husbands with no independent legal persona.[19] From the early thirteenth century on, most of a woman's property—whether inherited, purchased or earned—passed to her husband when she married. A wife could maintain legal ownership of land or other real property such as a house that she had before marriage, but its management came under her husband's control. She could not sell, rent, mortgage, gift or bequeath it without his consent. True, a husband was obligated to provide for his wife while he lived and to endow her with a share sufficient to maintain her for her "natural life" if she survived him. In essence, however, a married woman lost rights over her own property and earnings that were readily granted to single women and to widows.

The English aristocracy discriminated against their womenfolk even more harshly. Long after the 1540 Statute of Wills reestablished testamentary freedom for real property—indeed, well into the twentieth and even the twenty-first centuries—the upper classes continued to pass on their estates and titles to the first-born (or oldest surviving) son. Primogeniture was not a law, however, except in cases of intestacy: rather, it was a Norman *custom* descending from feudal times. Nor was it just any custom: rather, it was a formidable social institution designed to perpetuate the dynastic inheritance of landed estates, wealth, political power, social status, and cultural privilege among elite families. [20]

What happens when there are no sons to inherit? Could daughters take their place? No. Consider the drama of the British television series *Downton Abbey*.

It is 1921. Robert Crawley, the fictional seventh Earl of Grantham and the father of three daughters but no sons with his American wife Cora, has just heard the news. Patrick Crawley, the son of Robert's first cousin, the closest male descendant of Robert's grandfather (the "nearest agnate" of the Roman Twelve Tables!) and thus heir presumptive of Downton Abbey, the earldom and the family fortune, has sunk into the seas with the Titanic. Who, then, is next in line to inherit? Tracing back through the male bloodline to a common *great* grandfather, it is discovered to be Robert's third cousin once removed: the as yet unknown—but fortunately handsome and unmarried—Matthew Crawley.

What accounts for this odd state of affairs? As was the custom among the landed gentry, Downton Abbey is *entailed,* or legally encumbered. A binding document drawn up by the first Earl stipulates that the estate must pass down "in perpetuity" through the eldest son of the eldest son, or, failing that, through a younger son in the male line. Daughters cannot inherit because their shares would go to their husbands when they married. (Indeed, the considerable fortune that Robert's wife Cora Levinson brought with her into the marriage has vanished with her husband's bad investments, a situation of which she has been kept completely unaware.) The crisis of succession is averted when Robert and Cora's oldest daughter, Lady Mary, agrees to marry Matthew. The timely arrival of baby George through Matthew's bloodline ensures that the estate and title will stay in the family at least one more generation.

English settlers arriving in the American colonies during the seventeenth and eighteenth centuries came from both common and aristocratic stock. As such, they brought with them very different orientations toward inheritance. Whereas farmers settling on small to medium-size family holdings in New England and the Middle Atlantic typically exercised their customary testamentary freedom by giving their property to sons and/or daughters as they wished, wealthy families in the Southern Atlantic colonies whose plantations depended on slave labor generally willed their estates to the oldest son, following the custom of the English landed gentry.[21]

Intestacy rules across the colonies reflected these differences. Before 1776, the statutes of nine of the sixteen colonies—all of them in New England or the Middle Atlantic—specified that the property of the deceased (subject to the rights of the surviving husband or wife) must be distributed to *all* of his children, regardless of sex and birth order.[22] (Some colonies modified the rules by assigning double portions for the oldest son and/or half portions—or less—for daughters.) The five Southern colonies plus Rhode Island and New York mandated primogeniture, as was still the legal default in England.[23] Just as today, the rules depended on the state in which you lived.

Following the American Revolution, all of the original colonies (now states) were quick to abolish the systems of entails and primogeniture in intestacy cases, at least in principle. (A testator could still set up a trust preserving control over transfers to future generations). In 1777, Georgia became the first state to terminate both customs in its new constitution; in 1791, South Carolina was the last of the original states to do so. From then on, the property of a man who died without a valid will would be partitioned *equally* among his legitimate children, both male and female. A widow would receive a child's share or the return of the dower she brought into the marriage (if it was still intact), at her option.[24]

Historians note that entails and primogeniture had not been popular in most of the colonies, however, or even necessary. For one thing, land was plentiful. For another, the more visionary of the country's founders were eager to end such practices as part of the Great Experiment in establishing the new republic. As Jans Beckert explains,

> Many political leaders of the American Revolution believed that precisely the institutions of entailment and primogeniture succession were partly responsible for the social and political conditions in Europe they rejected, which is why they saw their abolition in America as an urgent task."[25]

It wasn't only in the United States that these radical changes were underway. With the enactment in 1804 of the Napoleonic Code (*Code Civil*) following the French Revolution, the French government ended both primogeniture and hereditary nobility. The Code's influence quickly spread to other areas under Napoleon's control in Western, Central and Southern Europe, an influence that is still felt today.

Unlike the Anglo-American system of testamentary freedom, however, the French Code required that all legitimate children (both female and male) receive equal shares of the estate, *will or no will.* All French male citizens were to have equal rights. Women could inherit, but they would remain legally subordinate to their fathers and husbands. Indeed, it would be many years before married women won the right to manage (and thus to bequeath) their own property in France—and in Britain and the United States as well.

Whereas primogeniture and entailments were abolished soon after American independence, the provisions of English

Common law relating to married women's property held fast for another fifty to one hundred years. We don't have to look very far to see how these worked. Presidents George Washington and Thomas Jefferson, for example, both owned large estates that depended on enslaved domestic, agricultural and artisanal workers. They owned other real estate and business shares as well. But what did their wives or daughters own?

It is 1799. With no children of his own, George Washington is writing his will at Mount Vernon. He bequeaths most of his extensive real and personal property there and elsewhere to his "dearly beloved wife, Martha Washington," for her "use, profit, and benefit...*for the term of her natural life.*" (Like the Dowager Countess of Downton Abbey, she may remain on the estate until she dies.) But what does Martha inherit to pass on in *her* will? The landholdings she brought into the marriage as a wealthy young widow with two children have (like Cora Levinson's fortune) been absorbed into her husband's estate.[26] In return, he writes,

> My improved lot in the Town of Alexandria, situated on Pitt and Cameron Streets, I give to her & her heirs forever, as I also do my household and kitchen furniture of every sort and kind, with the liquors and groceries which may be on hand at the time of my decease..."[27]

One-quarter of a century later, the widower Thomas Jefferson is writing *his* will in the year 1826 at Monticello. Having advocated for the abolition of primogeniture and entails in Virginia decades earlier, Jefferson now faces a different challenge. To make sure that the property he leaves to his only legitimate child, a daughter, will not fall into her husband's hands, he puts it in trust. But here's the catch: she must be widowed before she can claim it.

> Considering the insolvent state of affairs of my friend & son
> in law...I do hereby devise and bequeath all the residue of my
> property real and personal...*in trust*, for the sole and separate
> use...of my dear daughter Martha Randolph and her heirs...
> [such that] *at the death of my said son in law*...possession and use
> become vested in my said daughter and her heirs, in absolute
> property for ever.[28]

By the 1840s, challenges by women's rights advocates to the restrictive laws were beginning to bear fruit. During the next four decades, one by one, legislatures across the expanding American states passed Married Women's Property Acts protecting wives' ownership rights. Canadian provinces were passing similar laws. Following years of agitation in England, the British Parliament in 1880 enacted the Married Women's Property Act and broadened it two years later. Considered together, writes historian Carole Shammas, these Acts embodied "*the most substantial change in women's legal status in 700 years of the common law.*"[29]

And so it was that by the end of the nineteenth century, married women in every state of the union had won the right to manage, enjoy the profits, sell *and will* both personal and real property that they owned prior to marriage or had been given or inherited from a third party during marriage. Some states added protections for a wife's earnings from wage work or a business as well. The community property systems of seven Spanish-influenced western states and territories entering the union allocated to women not only the right to their separate property, as in common law jurisdictions, but a claim to half of the property acquired with their husbands during the marriage as well.[30]

We might expect that the passage of the Acts in the United States would have produced a surge of married women writing wills. But the new entitlements were not retroactive. Because they applied only to new marriages, their impact would not be felt for decades.[31] Another fly remained in the ointment as well. In both common law and community property states, husbands retained the right to administer assets accumulated *during* the marriage, his and hers. It would take many more decades of feminist advocacy before this proviso was overturned.[32]

Nevertheless, married women were emerging from the shadows of their husbands and into the light. In addition to their property rights, intestacy laws in the United States were also being rewritten to favor larger settlements on surviving spouses. Up to the late nineteenth century, wives' inheritance claims in both law and practice could best be described as "unequal and patriarchal" and the welfare of widows as "an afterthought."[33] A surviving wife might claim maintenance, but not a share of the marital property. The transformation since then has been extraordinary. As attorney Mark Accettura observes,

> In a little more than a century, wives have gone from a peripheral, or minor, legatee to a husband's primary beneficiary. Today, married decedents tend to leave everything to their spouse...[34]

What we do with our testamentary freedom and what the rules decree in intestacy cases are loosely intertwined. As the treatment of wives and widows shows, intestacy statutes in the United States have adapted themselves to changing norms and beliefs in ways that both *reflect* and *influence* what we consider normal and fair in bequeathing our assets within the family.

"But what was the Family?" Henry Maine asked of the Romans. How intestacy laws decide this question varies widely from state to state. [35] The American Bar Association points out that they have one thing in common: virtually all of them presume that our surviving spouse, if we have one, and our closest blood relatives will inherit our property after we die.[36] Most do not recognize in-laws (including spouses of our predeceased children) as family, nor stepchildren (usually), nor unmarried partners (except where states accept common-law marriages or civil unions). But they do now recognize married same-sex partners as well as children born outside of marriage, "relatives of the half blood" (children with one but not both parents in common), and children born from assisted reproduction, as long as there is a genetic connection.

In the absence of a valid will, the probate courts of each state designate beneficiaries based on rules that reflect a decedent's *presumed intent,* that is, on a statutory social standard of what is generally considered fair, just, and responsible. They do not and cannot attempt to determine our *actual intent,* however, whatever that might have been.[37] Thus, with few exceptions, an unmarried partner will not inherit, nor will exes, steps, in-laws, best friends, caregivers, domestic employees, business associates or charitable organizations. If we leave no spouse or children, the court's search for beneficiaries extends to living parents, siblings, grandparents, aunts and uncles, nieces, nephews and even beyond, as long as the bloodlines connect. If none can be traced, property reverts to the state (or, in feudal times, to a lord) by *escheat.*

In an attempt to achieve more uniformity and predictability across the states, the National Conference of Commissioners on Uniform State Laws in 1969 created a Uniform Probate Code that has been revised several times since then.[38] (There is also a Model Marital Property Act.) Annotated revisions are attributed to two main sources: first, changing social policies and practices in American society such as the rise in multiple marriages, blended families, and non-traditional forms of partnership, reproduction and parenting; second, the findings of research on what Americans think is fair.

Some inheritance studies ask respondents to say what they think an appropriate distribution would be in hypothetical family scenarios.[39] Others ask them to rate the fairness of certain entitlements in their state's intestacy laws and to give reasons for their objections, if any. An Ohio study questioned a sample of heirs who were identified from probate records. Eighty percent of the heirs of decedents survived by both spouse and children who had *written a will* reported that the distribution was "completely fair." Only 38 percent of survivors of decedents with spouse and children who *died intestate* said the distribution was completely fair, however, while 40 percent insisted it was "not fair" at all.[40] As far as fairness goes, the wills win.

Just as changing social norms and perceptions of fairness in the American population shape our intestacy laws, so, too, the laws themselves can influence the choices *we* make. It's not that most of us are familiar with our state laws, although it would behoove us to learn what they are. Rather, legal advisors may urge us to follow them:

> The main purveyors of the rules are estate planning and elder law attorneys who advise their clients on expectations and fairness. Clients often query whether they should leave to in-laws and stepchildren. They quickly decide against such bequests when they learn that *it is not the American custom to do so…*[41]

Does this mean that custom trumps freedom? Generally, yes, but not always. On the one hand, we have internalized as "natural" and "fair" a centuries-old heritage of individual freedoms that grant us the right to bequeath our possessions to whomever we wish. On the other hand, as members of society we are imbued with social customs and traditions favoring certain categories of recipients, such that our choices are almost predetermined. As historian Carole Shammas points out, "Americans have whenever possible limited their substantial bequests to spouse, sons, and daughters." Moreover, of testators who have children, 90 percent or more have passed up legacies to relatives, friends, and charities.[42]

Like the ancient Romans, then, it appears that we use our individual freedom not so much to disinherit a family member or to make an "unequal distribution of patrimony" (although this certainly happens, as we shall see). Rather, we use it primarily to fulfill social expectations of what is just and fair as adapted to our own point of view.

Writing a personal will may result in the unfair exclusion of deserving persons—at least from some perspectives—due to the testator's animosity or for some other reason. But by the same account, *not* writing a will may result in the unfair inclusion of undeserving persons such as an absentee parent, abusive spouse, or even a distant relative whom the deceased had never met. It can also result in the exclusion of deserving ones who might otherwise have been "remembered" in a will such as a domestic partner or caregiving daughter-in-law. Whether we intend to or not, these are the choices we make.

What happens when there is no choice? The testamentary freedom that we enjoy in the United States along with other countries such as Canada and Australia that share a heritage of English common law[43] is perched on a legal foundation of *forced heirship*, otherwise known as "protected heirship" or "forced succession". But whereas forced heirship applies to us only if we die without leaving a valid will,[44] in many countries—especially those influenced by the French *Code Civil* but also in countries with Islamic jurisdictions—it is the law of the land, *regardless of what one might wish.*[45] How does this work?

The laws of forced succession vary in important ways from country to country. Some civil codes exempt a discretionary portion of the estate from mandated distribution, for example. They also follow somewhat different rules of succession and distribution with respect to children, spouses and other kin. A person might get around the laws by transferring money or real estate during his or her lifetime, say, or signing a marriage contract, or setting up a foreign trust. But the common element is this:

> Under forced heirship rules, a person is not free to dictate who will inherit their estate. Instead, forced heirship laws require a deceased person's estate to pass to one or more blood relatives (usually children and grandchildren) and/or a surviving spouse, who are referred to as the "protected heirs.[46]

France represents an extreme version of this system. The 1804 Napoleonic Code, which remains largely extant, *guarantees* portions of an estate to specific heirs. One cannot leave everything to a charity or to someone outside the family circle, nor can one treat one's children unequally.[47] Because an estate must exceed a minimum value before a discretionary portion kicks in, only the wealthy (or those who are childless) are likely to write a personal will. Whereas two-thirds of Americans die having left a will, fewer than 10 percent of the French do so.[48]

The French Code was implemented in a number of European and Latin American countries during the nineteenth century. But its influence diminished following enactments of the German and Swiss Civil Codes in 1900 and 1912, both of which incorporated their own definitions of "rightful heirs."[49] While lineal descent prevailed, the treatment of spouses differed.[50] And for those who died with neither spouse nor direct descendants, their property would go to blood relatives in a fixed order of ascent (to parents or grandparents) or, if none survived, laterally to siblings (or cousins) and by descent to their offspring.

None of the civil codes permits the explicit disinheritance of children or grandchildren, which remains "one of the most important peculiarities of American inheritance law."[51] As Karl Marx explained of the English common law in an 1861 letter to his French colleague Ferdinand LaSalle "…by '*testamentary freedom*' I didn't mean freedom to make a will, but freedom to make it with complete disregard for one's family."[52] In writing their own civil code, German jurists also deemed testamentary freedom "too individualistic" and destructive of the social relations of family and society. Rejecting the personal will as an "alien element," they saw landowners as *trustees* of property that rightfully belongs not to individuals but to the family as a whole.[53]

The French *Code Civil* and other European adaptations undoubtedly resolved the confusion of multiple laws and local practices that preceded them.[54] But in declaring the rules of succession and distribution as fixed social policy, they abrogated the freedom of individuals to pass on their assets according to their own social conscience to beneficiaries such as non-family members and charitable organizations. Whereas the intestacy statutes in the United States based on English common law correspond to what lawmakers believe a reasonable testator would decide if he or she had made a will—that is, what is *customary* for most folks to do—the civil (and religious) codes lay down inheritance rules that individuals not only ought to but *must* follow in the interests of a social policy that safeguards the common good.

B ut what *is* the "common good"? Individual freedom or social responsibility? Should the government dictate who within the family inherits shares of the estate when someone dies, or should that be left to the testator to decide? Should a government tolerate or even facilitate the uninterrupted intergenerational flow of wealth within families, or should it intercede with the purpose of redistributing wealth from one generation to the next? The distinction is a highly ideological one, the former reflecting a particularly American notion of individualistic free enterprise, it would seem, and the latter a particularly European notion of a democratic socialist state.

Complex questions of fairness and justice surface when we confront these issues. Is testamentary freedom fair, for example? Some would say *no*, not if dependents and other family members are left destitute, if children are treated unequally (or disinherited), or if a surviving spouse gets everything (or not enough), and so on.

Is forced heirship fair? Some would say *no*, not if money and personal effects end up in the hands of heirs whose eligibility rests solely on their blood ties rather than on the "natural affections" or personal obligations of the deceased.

Is inheritance *itself* fair? Some would say *no*, not if the practice perpetuates social and economic inequalities in a society whose founders, by rejecting hereditary privilege, hoped to build a republic ensuring equal opportunity for all.

What, then, *is* fair or just when it comes to the institution of family inheritance? From what ideological perspective is this to be judged? We turn to these questions next.

CHAPTER TWO

IS INHERITANCE FAIR?
WHEN PRINCIPLES COLLIDE

> There might be little wrong with inherited wealth if we all
> received something approaching an equal share. But obviously
> we do not: inherited wealth is an issue because it is so massively
> unequal, reproducing social inequalities across generations.[55]

Inheritance is a fact of life. Each of us inherits many things at our birth and throughout our lifetimes. We inherit the genes of our biological parents and more distant forebears, for example, which configure our physical appearance and contribute to our intelligence, talents, temperament, proneness to certain diseases, and other traits. We inherit our "social capital," the product of parental (and, more broadly, familial and societal) investments in our socialization, skills acquisition, formal education, and other efforts to mold us into acceptable—and perhaps even valuable—members of society.

We inherit—for better or for worse—the constellation of family relationships into which we are born and grow up, plus a cultural heritage and identity, an assemblage of habits and norms and beliefs, a "mother tongue." We may also inherit—in the form of *inter vivos* gifts from parents or other relatives during their lifetimes—assets such as a down payment on a house, a car, jewelry, antiques or money, and a safety net that allows us to take risks. And, at the death of our parents or grandparents, or perhaps a stepparent, uncle or aunt, the more fortunate among us may inherit substantial real and personal property.

All of these modes of inheritance derive from the accident of our birth and from the intergenerational transfer of social and material wealth during our lifetimes. All shape who we are, what we may become, and what we have to pass on. And all serve to broaden or limit our opportunities as individuals, to reinforce social rankings, and to perpetuate the inequalities among us.

When we ask "Is inheritance fair?" then, our first response is, *Life itself is not fair.* Nor is inheritance fair, in its broadest interpretation.

And so we narrow the question to the process by which we pass on our worldly goods within the family at our death. Is the system itself fair? From whose perspective do we judge? What do the concepts of justice and fairness tell us about inheritance in American society today?

> When people differ over what they believe should be given or when decisions have to be made about how benefits and burdens should be distributed among a group of people, questions of justice or fairness inevitably arise.[56]

No doubt we would all agree with this observation. But what is considered "fair" or "just" as a general rule, or in particular circumstances, is subject to some dispute. Moreover, each of us is likely to bring our own perspectives to these issues, especially when they affect us in personal ways.

Definitions of justice and fairness are not necessarily helpful, for they can be abstract, elusive, and even circular. *What's fair is fair,* some say:

> *Distributive justice* refers to the extent to which society's institutions ensure that benefits and burdens are distributed among society's members in ways that are *fair and just*.[57]

Philosophers and political economists since the ancient Greeks have struggled with questions of distributive justice and how it is to be achieved. As early as the fourth century BCE, Plato declared that no one should be more than four times richer than the poorest member of the society.[58] Writing in the seventeenth to nineteenth centuries, theorists such as Thomas Hobbes, John Locke, Jean-Jacques Rousseau, Emmanuel Kant, and John Stuart Mill—and, more recently, John Rawls and others in the twentieth—contend that, as "rational individuals," we could—hypothetically, at least—rise above our self-interests and adopt a set of guiding principles to ensure the common good. But what, exactly, *is* the common good, and from whose points of view are such principles to be judged?

As "society's members" we are all a part of the "common," as in "common good." But each of us occupies a unique location within the whole according to our class position and social circumstances, our racial and ethnic identities, age, gender, family status, geographical location, and other personal and social characteristics. Our location relative to others in these hierarchical and overlapping networks carries enormous implications for our wellbeing and perspective on life. It is bound to influence our point of view about what's fair. Is the highly skewed distribution across American households of "benefits and burdens" and of wealth and opportunity fair, for example? Is it fair that some people inherit money "effortlessly" and others get nothing?

Definitions of fairness and justice can also be contradictory:

Fair: equitable; free from bias, dishonesty or injustice; legit-
imately performed under the rules or standards*; just or
appropriate* in the circumstances; *treating people equally* without favoritism or discrimination; impartial, unprejudiced,
honest.[59]

Justice means *giving each person what he or she deserves* or, in more
traditional terms, giving each person his or her due. [60]

But here's the dilemma: treating people equally is different from giving individuals "their due." How do we decide what each person or
group of people deserves? Is it possible to be impartial in making
such judgments? What *are* the rules or standards that are "appropriate in the circumstances"?

Let's begin with private property itself. Should it be distributed
equally? According to what each of us "deserves"? According to whatever we can accumulate by our own efforts, or the efforts of others? By the vagaries of chance or fortune? Each of these alternatives
brings a different principle to bear on how we think about inherited
wealth.

Individual ownership and accumulation of property is as American
as apple pie. Indeed, Thomas Jefferson's assertion of a right to
"life, liberty, and the pursuit of happiness" in the Declaration of
Independence is interpreted by some historians to refer to a right to
own and enjoy real and personal property. Others insist that "happiness" in this context represents the civic virtues of moderation and
justice in a free society.[61] In any case, for Jefferson, the broad *diffusion*

of private property rather than its concentration was a precondition for the establishment of a just and truly "republican" social order.[62]

A Constitutional right to property would have been clearer if James Madison had had his way. On June 8, 1789, Madison asked Congress to insert a Preamble to the Constitution stating that "Government is instituted and ought to be exercised for the benefit of the people; which consists in the enjoyment of life and liberty, *with the right of acquiring and using property*, and generally of pursuing and obtaining happiness and safety."[63] Although the inelegantly phrased language failed to pass Congress, the sentiment prevails.

Whatever the intention of the founding fathers, the American celebration of private property (and of private enterprise) as an inalienable right is expressed in our rejection not only of the feudal entitlements of monarchs, landed aristocracy and the church, but also of claims of the state. Indeed, the idea that government might own the means of production (even of essential industries or services) is anathema to most Americans.

The difficulty here is that the American belief that owning as much property as we can accrue is an individual *right* is on a collision course with an equally compelling American belief that all persons are (or should be) equal under the law and have (or should have) equal opportunities to succeed in life. As a consequence, we are faced with the challenge of trying to overlay a principle of fairness—*equal opportunity*—on a fundamentally *unequal distribution* across individuals and households of tangible and intangible property and of the privilege and power that such ownership entails.

Inheritance of family wealth clearly reinforces these inequalities. Yet, as the authors of *Inheritance and Wealth in America* point out, Americans are ambivalent about inheritance:

On the one hand, they seem to enthusiastically embrace an ideology of individual opportunity based on merit.... On the other hand, Americans simultaneously endorse the right of individuals to bequeath estates to their designated heirs as they see fit.... These contradictory ways to distribute valued resources pose a fundamental dilemma between freedom of choice at the individual level and equality of opportunity at the societal level."[64]

Principles of fairness and justice derive from multiple ideologies that have evolved throughout history in interaction with fundamental changes in the way societies are organized. It is thus not surprising that the principles themselves are often on a collision course, not only with other ideologies but also with their own internal inconsistencies. As Nobel-Prize-winning economist Amartya Sen explains, "There can be serious differences between competing principles of justice that survive critical scrutiny and can have claims to impartiality."[65] In other words, it's simply not the case that one set of principles necessarily incorporates reason, impartiality and fairness while others do not.

Sen offers three principles as examples. Each could be considered fair and impartial while producing very different outcomes. The first is that resources should go to those who can make good use of them ("effective use and utility"); the second, to those who produced them ("entitlement to the fruits of one's labor"); and the third, to those who currently are without ("economic equity and distributive fairness").[66]

All of these principles come into play when we decide how to distribute our goods within the family, as we shall see. But they are also relevant here, given that competing principles of justice also demand what Sen calls "different institutional arrangements in society" in order to manage individual and group claims to society's resources.[67]

C onflicting principles or ideologies of fairness shape our opinions about what role the intergenerational transmission of property plays (or should play) in American society today. Consider two broad points of view. The first sees passing on family wealth as freedom, reward and security; the second sees it as unearned wealth and unfair advantage.

Proponents of the first point of view see the ownership of private property as virtually *sacrosanct*: a "natural" (or even God-given) right and/or a constitutionally guaranteed individual liberty. Real and personal property is thus ours to accumulate, to buy and sell, to enjoy, to inherit, and to pass on as we wish. At the end of our lives, our final resolve regarding its disposition should be respected and complied with.

Acquiring wealth to pass on to one's heirs is also embraced as both incentive and reward for *individual initiative*. Working hard, husbanding one's resources, and investing wisely are said to benefit not only individuals and families but also the common good, the latter by fostering an industrious ("virtuous") civil society. According to this logic, abolishing or restricting hereditary transmission would undermine the economic order and lower productivity by reducing people's incentives to work, save and invest.

Inheritance in this view also symbolizes *security*: security of the family and of existing property arrangements and expectations, both of which contribute to the common good. Investing in the wellbeing of children and grandchildren through *inter vivos* gifts and inheritances is an expression of family values directed toward securing the social standing, economic security and happiness of succeeding generations.

In this sense, inheritance is a *family legacy*, a gift from the deceased to be managed wisely and passed down through the generations. It is a symbol not only of achievement but also of family solidarity, continuity and love. Any intervention by the state in the form of taxation or other requirements at the time of a family member's death is said to be a particularly egregious affront to our rights and sensibilities.

From this perspective, then, all attempts to infringe on property rights or on the intergenerational transmission of family wealth are unfair. Private property must remain inviolable and the integrity of the family respected. Individuals must be free to distribute their wealth as they wish. "Death taxes" are unfair, immoral and inefficient—not to mention coercive—and their redistributive justification (if any) should be challenged. Why, some ask, should our hard-earned money go to people who haven't worked for it, that is, to the "undeserving poor"?[68]

The second point of view, which sees inheritance as inherently unfair, is clearly an opposing one. But it, too, draws on principles of social justice as its rationale.

Our forefathers abolished hereditary titles and the blatantly unfair semi-feudal arrangements of landed estates as portrayed in the novels of Jane Austin and the drama of Downton Abbey. But, proponents charge, the very existence of inherited wealth in the United States today violates principles of justice and fairness that underlie the American ideal of equality of *opportunity*, at the least, and most certainly of equality of *result*.

The very advantages of inheritance attributed to individuals, families, and the common good cited in the previous arguments are transmuted in this point of view to examples of distributive injustice, that is, as *violations* of individual rights and of the common good. Proponents argue that inherited wealth abuses the principle that everyone should have an equal opportunity to succeed in life according to his or her own efforts. Those who inherit wealth clearly have more opportunities and more protection from risk than those who do not.

Writing in the nineteenth century, the French philosopher and social reformer Henri de Saint-Simon contended that everyone has (that is, should have) a place in society according to his or her capacities; rewards should accrue in proportion to the work delivered.[69] The inheritance of property thus conflicts with the ideal of "to all people according to the productivity of their labor." (Note how this conflicts with yet another principle of fairness, the communist avowal of "*From* each according to his *ability, to* each according to his *need.*") Indeed, Saint-Simon contends that the only legitimate property right is based on the capacity to *use* the property, for example, to cultivate the land or to purchase tools of the trade. Existing property and inheritance rights should both be modified to reflect the value of work and productivity, he says, given that none of us has a right to property that we have not earned, to which we have not contributed, or which we are not putting to productive use.

From this point of view, then, inheritances represent unearned wealth. If recipients have done nothing to earn the money or improve the real property in question, then they have no right to it. Inherited wealth represents unfair competition with those who *are* productive. And because inheritance is matter of "luck" (an accident of birth) rather than a reward for our own hard work and/or careful investments, it is a social injustice that breeds resentment and alienation, especially among the poor and the working class.

As a mirror image of the incentive justification noted earlier, proponents of this point of view also argue that inheritance acts as a *disincentive* to individual initiative and saving—not for the testator whose bounty is passed on, but for the heirs who stand to benefit from it. Stories abound of second- and third-generation heirs who draw on trust funds or expectations of lump sum payments to live in a manner antithetical to the values and habits of those who built the fortunes. (This may not always be a bad thing, however, depending on how the fortunes were made. But that is another story.) "Family money" thus becomes not a valued legacy to be protected and passed on, but rather, a windfall to the "underserving rich."

In essence, the argument goes, the unrestricted intergenerational transfer of family wealth in and of itself is simply not fair. Progressive taxation or even outright limitation of such transfers at the time of death is needed to prevent the formation of financial dynasties (an oligarchy of wealth), abolish hereditary distinctions and privileges, require people to rely on their own efforts and achievements, and give everyone a fair and equal start in life.[70]

I n their book *Inherited Wealth, Justice and Equality,* John Cunliffe and Guido Erreygers remark that in both our own Anglo-Saxon common law traditions and in the continental civil codes,

> [T]he transmission of property by bequest was considered a matter of political and legal convention rather than an expression of some basic right to private property. Even if that right were recognized legally during the lifetime of property holders, it did not extend to the posthumous disposition of their holdings...[71]

As a matter of political decision-making and legal convention, then, inheritance in this context should be addressed *pragmatically* as a public policy issue rather than as an expression of some basic right to private property. The rules, in other words, can be changed. But how?

There are several possibilities. Assuming political will, the state could, for example, place absolute limits on the size of inheritances and lifetime gifts that any one person is allowed to receive. John Stuart Mill proposed this idea in the nineteenth century as a compromise between the principles of individual freedom, on the one hand, and social equality on the other. The state, he argued, should limit not what one can *bequeath*, "but what any one should be permitted to *acquire*, by bequest or inheritance.[72]

Inheritance itself would not be abolished, in Mill's view. Instead, a lifetime limit would be placed on the amount that any person could receive through family bequests and gifts, with the exception of spouses and minor children.[73] Assets would pass to those who have not exceeded their quotas, to charitable organizations that are exempt from quotas, or to the government in the form of taxation. Testators would be motivated to make bequests to persons other than those they have previously endowed, such as siblings, grandchildren, nieces and nephews, employees, friends, or charities, thus spreading the wealth. In intestacy cases, Mill contends that only the spouse and minor children should have a right to inherit, and then only what they need to avoid being a burden on society. The rest would transfer to the public good.[74]

Alternatively, and more realistically, the state can levy taxes on large *estates*, to be paid off the top before assets are distributed to beneficiaries; on *inheritances*, to be paid on receipt by individual beneficiaries; and on *inter vivos* gifts to adult children, especially those made "in anticipation of death."[75] Economist Pierre Pestieau submits that taxes on *estates*, which characterize systems of testamentary freedom as found in England and the United States, are more efficient but less equitable than are taxes on *inheritance*, which characterize systems of forced succession and equal distribution among children in the French *Code Civil* and elsewhere in continental Europe.[76]

British economist Anthony Atkinson brings a contemporary perspective to bear on Mill's ideas on inheritance. In his book *Inequality: What Can Be Done?* Atkinson presents ten proposals for reducing economic inequality in Britain and the United States.[77] Proposal Ten is this: "Receipts of inheritance and gifts *inter vivos* should be taxed under a progressive lifetime capital receipts tax." Preferring this "lifetime capital receipts tax" to a burdensome single-year inheritance tax, Atkinson quotes Mill's idea of "a heavy graduated succession duty on all inheritances exceeding [a] minimum amount which is sufficient to aid but not supersede personal exertion."[78] (Presumably this graduated tax would reach 100 percent when absolute limits were reached.) Heirs could reduce their marginal tax rate by giving to charity. Testators, in turn, could pass on all of their assets tax free to heirs who have received little so far in lifetime receipts, thus helping to reduce gender and generational inequalities.

On the surface, all of these models of taxation appear to offer a fair and reasonable means of redistributing wealth and raising revenue for the state. They seem fair because they are targeted toward those with greater wealth. They seem reasonable because they permit substantial intergenerational transfers while extracting some for the public good.

But here's the rub: the majority of Americans disagree with this assessment. Americans tend to hurl charges of unfairness at the government's collection of so-called "death taxes" with greater vehemence than at any other form of taxation. And we do this despite the fact that very few of us will end up paying any estate or inheritance taxes at all.

When asked which of four federal taxes is "the worst tax—that is, *the least fair*" (emphasis added)—respondents to on-line polls sponsored by the Tax Institute in 2005 and 2006 were more likely to name the *estate tax* than the federal income tax, Social Security payroll tax, or corporate income tax.[79] (There is no federal inheritance tax or wealth tax.) Respondents would presumably hold the same or even more hostile views of the twelve states and the District of Columbia that also tax estates as well as the four that tax inheritances, not to mention the two (Maryland and New Jersey) that tax both.[80]

More than two-thirds of those taking the on-line poll favored *completely eliminating* the estate tax—"that is, the tax on property left by people who die." The aversion to estate taxes is not restricted to the United States, according to Jens Beckert's accounts of Germany and France and Pierre Pestieau's of Italy. But it is heartfelt. People tend to view estate taxes not only as "double taxation" but also as an unwarranted, immoral, and particularly ill-timed appropriation of wealth that should rightfully go to its designated heirs.

How many of us believe that we ourselves would benefit from ending the estate tax? Very few: only 17 percent in one Gallup poll.[81] But even this low figure greatly overestimates the number of us who would actually be affected. Of 2.6 million people who died in the United States in 2013, for example, the federal government levied taxes on only 4,700 estates, that is, on *fewer than 0.02 percent of the total.*[82]

In their book *Inheritance in America: From Colonial Times to the Present*, historian Carole Shammas and colleagues note that estate and inheritance taxes were instituted in some states as early as the eighteenth century.[83] In 1862, the U.S. Congress enacted a federal "duty or tax" to be imposed on certain types of property passing from the deceased by will or intestacy. The modern U.S. estate tax, first enacted by Congress in 1916, has gone through a number of revisions over the past century as the political winds and public opinion changed course. According to economists Thomas Piketty and Gabriel Zucman,

> One can...interpret the spectacular rise of tax progressivity that occurred in the United States during the first half of the twentieth century as an attempt to preserve the egalitarian, democratic American ethos (celebrated a century before by Tocqueville and others). *Attitudes toward inequality are dramatically different today.*[84]

Let's consider the evidence for this roller-coaster ride. In the 1930s and 1940s, roughly 1.5 percent of all decedents' estates were subjected to taxes. But in the postwar years, populist and progressive movements fueled support for higher levies.[85] Coverage jumped from 3 to over 7 percent of all estates in the 1950s through the 1970s, even as exemptions such as charitable donations were added for the wealthy.

By 1970, though, popular support for an estate tax was morphing into opposition, not only to a steeply progressive tax, but also to any federal estate tax at all.[86] Congressional action followed suit: the minimum value of estates immune from federal taxation rose steadily year by year, from $120,000 in 1977 to $325,000 in 1984 to $600,000 in 1987, where it remained until 1995.[87] Then it jumped again: by 2004-2005 the tax threshold had reached $1.5 million, rising every year up to $5.0 million for persons dying in 2011 and $5.490 million in 2017. And in December 2017, Congress doubled the exemption to almost $11 million—$22 million for married couples—with cost of living increases effective to the year 2025.[88]

The consequences of these legislative shifts are startling. The percentage of estates owing any federal taxes at all slid from 7.65 percent in 1976 to 0.88 percent in 1987 to under 0.02 percent as Congress added more and more exemptions, now including family foundations and all transfers to spouses.[89] Not only that, the top tax rate for the largest estates net of exemptions dropped from 55 percent in 2001 to 40 percent in 2016. As wealth is increasingly concentrated, the richest families pass on larger and larger amounts of their assets intact.[90]

I deally, a tax system should be *efficient* as measured by the ratio of costs to benefits, *effective* in achieving its specified goals, and *equitable* in its intent, implementation and outcomes.

We can question current inheritance-related tax policies with respect to each of these elements. Critics challenging the privileged tax status for transfers *within* the family, for example, suggest that estate taxes may not be the fairest or most effective approach to promoting a more egalitarian distribution of wealth as compared with inheritance taxes, say, or a truly progressive federal tax on incomes (including capital gains), capital transfers, or even on wealth itself.[91] "The various alternatives of taxation often appear unpredictable in their consequences, dilemmatic, contradictory, and problematic in some of their complex repercussions," observes Jens Beckert. Moreover,

... when it comes to political battles over distribution the actors involved cannot be made to embrace abstract principles of justice if their implementation can be expected to produce disadvantages for their own situation.[92]

Whatever the outcome, the crux of the matter is this: where the evidence of the effects of inheritance on the distribution of wealth across American households may point in one direction, our opinions about what is fair and what isn't tend to point in another.

For one thing, the principles that we cite (usually selectively) to defend or challenge particular practices are on a collision course with one another, as we have seen. For another, as "society's members" we are often unaware of the facts and/or are willing to tolerate a rather high (but comforting) level of cognitive dissonance in our views. In his article on economic equality in *Scientific American*, author Nicholas Fitz calls this "The great divide between our beliefs, our ideals, and reality."[93] Consider two examples.

First, we noted earlier that, whereas 17 percent of respondents in one set of surveys believe that they would benefit from abolishing the federal estate tax, only 0.02 percent of estates—two in ten thousand—actually owe any tax. Better information does make a difference: participants in one experiment who were given these facts beforehand were far more likely to say that the estate tax should be *increased* than those who were not given the facts (53 vs. 17 percent).[94] But even for those who believe that the rich should pay more, "most people see the money they've earned as theirs to spend or pass on to their children, if they choose to do so," writes Karlyn Bowman in *Forbes*. "They don't think government should be able to take it away when they die. When Americans hear about it, their basic sense of fairness is offended."

Second, most of us greatly underestimate the degree of wealth (and income) inequality in the United States today. Whereas the richest *fifth* of U.S. households in 2012 owned 84 percent of the wealth, respondents in one survey guessed on average that they owned 59 percent. And, whereas the bottom 40 percent owns a mere 0.3 percent of the country's wealth (many households have more debt than assets), respondents guessed 9 percent.[95] Economists remind us that the very richest American families—the top 0.1 percent, or one in one thousand—are fast pulling away from the pack. Claiming 7 percent of the wealth in the late 1970s, they now claim more than 22 percent, and their shares are rising fast.[96]

Americans do acknowledge that the gap between the rich and poor has widened over the last decade, says Nicholas Fitz.[97] But "very few see it as a serious issue. Just five percent of Americans think that inequality is a major problem in need of attention." Not only that: "*Although most Americans believe the economic system unfairly favors the wealthy, a majority believes that success is due largely to individual talent and effort and that most people can make it if they're willing to work hard*" (emphasis added). Fitz notes that this "distinctly American cultural optimism" leads us to ignore important social determinants of success, such as structural discrimination, social connections, and family inheritance.

E thical discourses, political disputes, reflections of philosophers, opinions of economists: all of these exchanges may seem distant and abstract to us when we sit down alone or with family members or professional advisors to formulate our estate plans.

But, wittingly or not, each of us is taking an ideological position when we do so. To whom does (or should) our real and personal property belong after we die? Should we pass everything on to our spouse and/or children (if we have any), even if they are already comfortably well off? Or should we extend the "natural objects of our bounty" to other beneficiaries in greater need of assistance or to organizations that contribute to the public good? Should we do everything we can to avoid paying taxes with the tools that estate planning books offer us to *Lower Your Overall Estate Tax Burden* and for *Holding On To as Much as You Can?*[98] Or should we willingly ante up our fair share if our wealth makes us eligible for that exclusive club? Whatever we decide, our choices will reflect on principles of fairness and justice, no matter how personal they may seem.

Earlier in this chapter we quoted the authors of *Inheritance and Wealth in America* who noted that Americans seem to enthusiastically embrace an ideology of individual opportunity based on merit while simultaneously endorsing the individual right to bequeath our estates as we see fit. "These contradictory ways to distribute valued resources pose a fundamental dilemma between freedom of choice at the individual level and equality of opportunity at the societal level," they conclude.[99]

But is this necessarily the case? Perhaps not. If, as testators, we "freely choose" to pass on our estates in ways that promote social justice, then the two goals could be reconciled, at least in our individual instances.

We know that equality of opportunity requires a reasonably level playing field, a starting point where the odds of success are not predetermined by the socioeconomic circumstances of the families into which we are born. But privilege reinforces privilege. As economist Anthony Atkins explains, "The beneficiaries of inequality of outcome today can transmit an unfair advantage to their children tomorrow." "If we are concerned about equality of opportunity tomorrow," he adds, "we need to be concerned about inequality of outcome today."[100] In other words, by favoring the less well off in our own bequests rather than passing on our wealth to those who have (or will have) plenty, we are benefiting not only the individuals or organizations that receive our gifts, but also the cause of social justice.

In the next chapter we take a closer look at how inequalities in the distribution of assets across households in the United States correlate with who gives and receives inheritances, and how much. We also look at gender-based inequalities in assets *within* households—that is, who owns what in a marriage that they can pass on in a will—as well as differences between the sexes in average life spans and their implications for transfers to surviving spouses and to the next generation. And finally, we do have evidence on charitable giving. Who gives more and who gives less? What's fair and what's not from the perspectives of the family members involved and the larger ethical issues that arise?

CHAPTER THREE

INHERITANCE IN THE UNITED STATES: EXPECTATIONS, ASSETS, INEQUALITIES

Melody was just sixteen when Leonard Plumb Sr. decided to establish a trust for his children.... The funds, Leonard Sr. explained, would not be available until Melody, the youngest, turned forty. Jack was the first to argue vociferously against this distribution, wanting to know why they all couldn't have their share sooner and pointing out that Melody would get the money earlier in her life than everyone else and *what was fair about that?*[101]

Many of us will collect an inheritance—however small—at some point in our lives. Both the monetary value and the timing of what we receive are highly uncertain, as we learn in the tale of Leonard Plumb Sr. and his children in Cynthia Sweeney's novel, *The Nest.* But despite these uncertainties, two of every three Baby Boomers—the generation born between 1945 and 1965 who are now in their fifties and sixties—can expect to receive at least one bequest from parents (the most likely), grandparents, aunts or uncles, or some other source.[102]

Marked social and economic inequalities underlie the chances of inheriting anything, of course. As we saw in Chapter Two, "There might be little wrong with inherited wealth if we all received something approaching an equal share."[103] But clearly we do not. A national survey by MetLife reports that one of every two among the poorest 10 percent of all U.S. households receives an inheritance.[104] The median value of bequests reported by these low-asset households is $8,000 (half receive more, half less) and the mean (average) is $27,000. In contrast, four of every five among the wealthiest 10 percent of households receives an inheritance, with a median value of $335,000 and a mean—pulled up by extremes at the top—of $1.5 million. Sharp racial differences underlie these patterns as well. Whites were five times more likely than African Americans in one survey to say they had inherited money, for example, and their typical inheritance was ten times larger.[105]

Not every rich household receives an inheritance nor does every poor household go without. Nevertheless, the rich get more (indeed, much, much more) and the poor get very little. This is an inevitable outcome of the highly skewed distribution of wealth across households in the United States which, despite our collective faith in the idea of equal opportunity, has been described as the "most unequal of all Western nations."[106]

What recipients *do* with their inheritances makes a difference too. Do most of us save or spend what we get? [107] This depends on how much we already have as well as on the emotional significance we attach to the bequest. If it's a family tradition, a legacy passed down from our grandparents' time or before, we might salt it away to pass on to our own children or, if we haven't any, to our siblings' offspring. Otherwise we might view a bequest as an opportunity to retire earlier, pay off a mortgage, help out our own children or grandchildren with school fees or a loan, or as a windfall to enjoy as we wish. If we're young when we receive it, or short of cash or the amount is small, we could spend it pretty quickly.

A national survey of late Baby Boomers who were in their forties and early fifties at the time found that married respondents and those with higher incomes and longer work histories were more likely to save their inheritances. Younger, lower income, and recently divorced respondents were more likely to spend or lose them.[108] What they did also depended on how much they received: inheritances of $10,000 or less went especially fast. It appears that the more we have already and the more we inherit, the more likely it is that a bequest will "stick," thus compounding the inequalities.

Most Boomers now in their fifth and sixth decades of life also anticipate *leaving* a bequest to younger generations. Among those who have more than $25,000 invested in equities in addition to other assets, for example, three-quarters say they are certain or have "some probability" of passing on $100,000 or more.[109] An additional one-quarter expects to leave less than this amount, while only a few are certain to leave nothing. Collectively, Boomers are anticipated to bequeath an estimated $30 trillion to their heirs.[110] Fortunately for the heirs, a far higher percentage of aging parents say they expect to leave an inheritance than their adult children expect to receive one.[111] But giving is uncertain. Assets may shift or lose value, debts may pile up, and expenses can escalate in the later years of life, especially for the elderly needing long-term care. Expectations are one thing: realities quite another.

What do we expect to be able to pass on when we die? Let's start with our *net worth*—that is, our "wealth" as it stands now.

This is the sum of the property that we own minus the debts that we owe. This may sound simple enough, but the types of assets that are included in these calculations and their fluctuating value (stock shares or real estate, for example) can complicate matters considerably. Moreover, the balance of assets and debts at our death might be very different from what it is when we're writing our will. This means that expectant heirs might well discover that a parent's estate is worth next to nothing despite what the parent had planned and wanted to give. Or they may find that it is worth far more than anyone guessed.

Useful modules for listing assets and debts can be found in some estate planning guides.[112] On the plus side is our *real property*, such as our home (primary residence, vacation home), other real estate (e.g., commercial and rental property), land, farm and heavy equipment, livestock, vehicles, a family business, bank accounts, stocks and bonds, and other assets with our name on the title or on the shares as owner or co-owner. These all count toward our net worth.

On the minus side is the money we owe: an outstanding mortgage, say, or a personal loan, credit card balance, car payment, taxes, or some other obligation. "Your debts don't die with you," the American Bar Association reminds us. "Your estate is still liable for them, and your executor has the authority and the duty to pay them off if they are valid and binding."[113] Personal debts will be taken out of our estate's assets before anything is given to our heirs. If debts exceed assets, the heirs will receive nothing and the creditors will collect a prorated share of what they are due.[114]

Our estate also consists of our *personal property* such as household furnishings, clothing, books, art works, jewelry, computers and mobile devices, special collections, memorabilia, antiques, and other possessions that we accumulate during our lifetimes. Not all of our real or personal property is passed on in our wills, however. Life insurance policies or bank and retirement accounts with designated beneficiaries go directly to the individuals named in the contract, or into a named trust for distribution at the time of our death. Property held in joint tenancy automatically passes to the surviving co-owner. Valuable items of personal property may be bequeathed to beneficiaries named in the will or in an attached tangible personal property memorandum but are otherwise left to family members to divide among themselves.

What do we own *personally* that is ours to bequeath if we're married? It's surprising to learn how many married people, especially wives, actually have no idea. What we own as individuals in a marriage is defined by the marital property laws of the state in which we reside. Fair or unfair, that's the way it is in our federal system. So, too, state statutes determine our legal status as a couple, which in turn establishes the validity of our claims. Registered marriages (conventional and same-sex) are recognized in all states; registered civil partnerships in most; "common law" marriages in which long-time cohabiting couples represent themselves as married in some; and "living together" in virtually none.[115]

When a married couple splits up, one or both partners may insist that what they get to *take away* from the union is not fair. The same applies to what partners can *give away* in a will, with one major qualification: couples in a first (but not necessarily a second or third) marriage are usually advised to leave everything to their surviving spouse. If this happens, the question of who owns what is pretty much irrelevant. In other situations, however, it can be critical.

As we saw in Chapter One, the legal system of the United States derives primarily from English common law as adapted in the colonies and across the states over the years since then. But we have inherited other systems as well. The marital property laws of nine states are grounded in the French civil code (Louisiana) and Spanish community property laws that were acquired or copied from the days when these territories belonged to other countries.[116]

Two distinct—and conflicting—sets of principles underlie the rules of marriage and property ownership in common law and community property states. Each could be declared as just or unjust depending on our personal situation and ideological point of view.

In the forty *common law* states (two have mixed arrangements) and the District of Columbia, all titled property (e.g., real estate, bank accounts, stocks shares, pensions, vehicles, a farm or business) belongs to the person or persons *whose name is on the title*. It is their separate property, regardless of who earned the money, who paid for it, or who worked for it. This "title-based" principle of ownership applies to everyone, irrespective of marital status. The titled owner can make whatever decisions he or she wishes about bequests. A court may order a richer spouse to turn over property to a poorer spouse in case of a divorce. But only if couples hold property in some form of shared ownership do they both have claims to it: a joint bank account with both names on it, for instance, or a house held in "tenancy in common" (each person owns an individual interest as separate property) or "joint tenancy with right of survivorship" (one owns it all when the other dies).[117]

Unless her name is on property titles along with her husband's, a wife in a common law state who has spent most of her married life at home raising children might well discover that she owns nothing of value to pass on in her will. Testamentary freedom means little in a situation such as this. If her husband dies first and she is in his good graces, she might inherit all his property, or a goodly share, which becomes hers to bequeath as she wishes. If she inherits little or nothing, she has the right to claim a statutory "elective share" of her husband's estate in court, typically one-third but perhaps more. (The same holds true for both spouses.) This right is based on the common law principle that spouses have mutual duties to support one another during their joint lifetimes and, to some extent, after death.[118]

Community property states are based on very different principles. Marriage is treated as a collaborative partnership and a joint economic endeavor. Both partners have equal rights to a half share of all income and property that either or both of them acquire during the marriage, that is, to the property of the two-person "community." These rights accrue to both partners *regardless of whose name is on the title* of the property (even a retirement account), who earns or pays, or who contributes labor, irrespective of the length of the marriage.

Married people in a community property state may also own separate property. Assets acquired by either of them before marriage plus subsequent income from or appreciation of these assets are separate, but only as long as they are not co-mingled later (e.g., not placed in a joint bank account). So, too, are inheritances or gifts that either receives during the marriage, with the same proviso. Typically, then, a married person in a community property state will own a half share of the community property and all of her or his separate property. These assets can be passed on in a will to whomever the testator wishes, such as the surviving spouse, children, other relatives, non-relatives or charitable organizations. A surviving spouse who is disinherited has no legal claim to anything, given that he or she already owns half of the community property.

Couples in community property states can override these arrangements by signing a prenuptial or postnuptial agreement with different terms. They can agree to maintain everything as separate property during the marriage, for example, as long as they keep individual accounts under their own names of their earnings, investments, property purchases, and so on. This is a preferred arrangement in a second or third marriage. Conversely, they may decide that some or all of what one or both brought into the marriage should belong to them equally (a house, for example), in which case they would sign an agreement to this effect.

Let's assume that whether we live in a common law or community property state, as a married person we are aware of (or will find out very soon!) what we own personally and can keep if we are divorced or give away to others now, later, or at our death. *What will we do with our testamentary freedom?* What do estate planners advise? What does our family expect? What role, if any, will principles of fairness or social justice play in the decisions we make?

"For the most part," says the American Bar Association, "what you put in your will is your decision."[119] We may leave everything or nothing to a spouse or intimate partner; to our children or grandchildren; to other family members (stepchildren, perhaps, or a niece or nephew); to friends, caregivers, a faithful employee; or to the Red Cross, Planned Parenthood, a church, university, hospital, animal shelter, community food bank, family foundation, or some other entity. Given all of this freedom, what do most of us do if we're married? It appears that almost all bequests from married couples go primarily to surviving spouses *even when there are grown children.* Indeed, attorneys may specifically recommend it:

Except where extenuating circumstances dictate, in first marriages one's surviving spouse should be named primary *and sole* beneficiary."[120]

Naming a spouse as sole beneficiary is a matter of custom rather than of law, however.[121] But there are monetary benefits as well: such transfers are exempt from federal estate taxes regardless of the amount.[122] The result is that husbands generally bequeath a larger share of their assets to their wives than most states would require if they were to die intestate.[123] Whereas widows in the late nineteenth century received far smaller shares of their husband's estate, they now typically receive 100 percent except for the wealthiest testators.[124] Not only that: in most contemporary wills, the surviving spouse is named as *both executor and beneficiary.*[125]

How many of us have a spouse, though, as we sail into our sunset years? According to the 2010 U.S. census, 79 percent of men and 56 percent of women ages sixty-five to seventy-four were currently married or in a recognized union. At age seventy-five and older, 70 percent of men but only 32 percent of women were still in a marriage, due mostly to the loss of a spouse. This means that in this oldest age group, *three-quarters of men but only one-third of women have a spouse* to whom they could leave their estate.

Should a surviving spouse necessarily get everything? Or should the size or proportion of the bequest depend on factors such as the length of the marriage, whether the spouse needs any or all of it, whether she or he is likely to remarry, and whether the testator would prefer to leave at least part of his or her estate to someone (or something) else?

Surviving spouses don't all belong to the First Wives' Club. According to one national survey, by their mid-forties only 50 percent of women who had ever married were still in their first marriage. Forty-six percent had divorced, and among those, two-thirds had remarried.[126] The divorce rate among people aged fifty and older doubled between 1990 and 2010 while the overall rate remained fairly flat.[127] At the same time, the proportions of older folks who are getting married again or just moving in together is on the rise.

These demographic trends mean that, at a time in our lives when we are most likely to be writing or updating our wills, we are even less likely to be in our first marriages and more likely to be remarried or widowed (if not separated, divorced or still single). Leaving everything to a surviving spouse when one has children from a previous marriage can be particularly unfair from the children's point of view. As the authors of *Family and Inheritance* found in the study of probated wills in Ohio, "Most of the feelings of unfairness in testate cases involving spouse and children were accounted for by the problems arising out of remarriage." This was particularly the case where the decedent's children saw everything pass to a stepparent, including the family home, financial assets, and the parent's personal possessions.[128] Attorney Richard Barnes warns of this unhappy outcome:

> The most common goal in estate planning for blended families is to provide for a surviving spouse, then benefit your children once your spouses passes.... You'll see that perhaps the most commonly used technique—making an outright gift to [a] surviving spouse—actually provides the least certainty that your children will ultimately end up with anything.[129]

The practice of leaving everything to a surviving spouse also has major implications for the value of the estate that is eventually passed on, its timing (considering our life spans), and the selection of beneficiaries. A testator may leave everything to a first or subsequent spouse in a will with no strings attached. Or, he or she may leave the estate to the surviving spouse in trust for the children. The grieving widow or widower may draw on the estate as needed to provide for her or his "comfort, welfare, and happiness" so long as the appointed trustee agrees. At the spouse's death the estate passes to the named beneficiaries.[130]

Hopeful heirs may be startled and dismayed to realize how long they might have to wait for their inheritance, however. "Leaving everything to a surviving spouse is a form of disinheritance that children of first marriages readily accept," one expert assures us.[131] But is this always true? If a parent truly needs it all, probably yes. But if there is enough to go around, perhaps not. For the middle generation now in their fifties or sixties, it's not just *whether* they are included in the will and *what* each of them will receive, but *when* they can expect to receive it that is likely to count from their perspective.

That more and more of us are living well into our nineties and beyond has enormous import for all three inheritance concerns of potential heirs: the whether, what, and when. Greater longevity means not only long delays in passing on the family estate, but also the possibility that its value will be diminished by the high costs of elder care or even vanish entirely.

Where a testator passes the entire estate to the spouse who is still living, the timing of adult children's inheritance is pushed back even further. "We'll be in our sixties or seventies by the time we receive our inheritance," complains one family member. "Dad left everything to Mom but she doesn't need it all to live on. Why didn't he leave some of it to us now, when we could really use it? After all, we have kids and grandkids ourselves!"

Consider our life spans. According to current life expectancies, a sixty-five-year-old woman can expect to live to age eighty-seven on average; a man to age eighty-four. Predictions are even higher for folks who've already reached age seventy-five: on average, they can expect to live to about eighty-nine and eighty seven, respectively.[132] But what if one spouse leaves everything to the other? The probabilities that *one* of them will live to a very old age as a "surviving spouse" are even more dramatic. If both partners are now sixty-five, for example, there is a 45 percent chance that *one of them* will live to age ninety or beyond.[133] And for partners who are now seventy-five, the chance that one of them will live to age ninety or more is 53 percent. These probabilities skyrocket if the wife is many years younger than her husband.

Life expectancies are uncertain, of course. Moreover, national averages obscure individual and group differences in health status and their connections with social, economic and cultural characteristics. How long we're likely to live is correlated with our household income, for example, and also with our geographical residence. And as is the case for the growing inequalities of wealth and income across American households, the rich have been adding more years to their life spans over the past two decades than the poor, and whites more than blacks.[134]

These predictions of longer life spans tell a compelling story. Unless we provide for our heirs in other ways, they may have to wait a very long time. And it's not only the longer wait for an inheritance that might seem unfair to grown children. It's also the prospect of a rapidly shrinking estate if elderly parents (or stepparents) draw down their capital for medical expenses and assisted living or nursing care. Even more alarming is the possibility that adult children may be called upon to pay. Estimates of remaining years of life, possible health care costs, and the amount likely to be covered by Medicare reveal major shortfalls for the elderly unless they have set aside considerable funds for their later years and have additional health coverage.[135]

Are children legally responsible for their elderly parents? Historians note that prior to the twentieth century "there was no question that a filial relationship defined a natural obligation" of child to parent.[136] However, commentators on the social and economic consequences of population aging note that older parents are less dependent on their grown children for support these days than they were previously, and are far less likely to live with their children. In 1900, for example, 61 percent of Americans aged sixty-five and over lived with adult children; in 1962, 25 percent; in 1975, 14 percent; presumably far fewer today.[137]

Changes in family ideologies are partly responsible for this shift. What we once viewed as filial obligations of children to parents are now more likely to be seen as the reverse.[138] Public policies such as pensions, Medicare and Social Security have lessened reliance of parents on children, along with the growth of alternative living and long-term care arrangements such as retirement communities and nursing homes. Although the laws of some states do require that children provide minimal support for indigent parents, these laws are rarely enforced except in a few places where nursing homes have brought lawsuits against the sons or daughters of patients who are unable to pay.[139]

Other scenarios can reduce the size of an estate, of course. As Shammas and her colleagues point out, while parental duty to provide for their children diminishes as they grow older, "parents also place less emphasis on saving to pass on to children, and more on providing a pleasant (and long) retirement for themselves and a secure future for the surviving spouse, most often the wife."[140] The surviving spouse—especially a husband—may also marry again, acquire stepchildren, and even start a new family if his new partner is much younger than he is.

All of these possibilities (and more) can create considerable anxiety among prospective heirs in the over-fifty "middle generation" and among their offspring as well. With testamentary freedom, grown children are not entitled to inherit anything from their parents nor are parents obliged to give them anything. But, entitled or not, they are likely to feel that they ought to receive *something* at the death of a parent—assuming there is something to leave—and that this "something" represents not just money, but also commitment and love. This is especially so in the case of a second marriage. Elder law attorney Mark Accettura has this advice for those who have remarried:

> Consider an outright transfer to natural children at the death of the first spouse in an amount that will not jeopardize the well-being of the surviving spouse. Parents who completely withhold all distributions to their children until after the death of a stepparent create a potential deathwatch among their own progeny waiting to receive what they believe to be rightfully theirs.[141]

To ensure that adult children receive assets immediately, estate planners suggest that they be designated as beneficiaries of life insurance policies or bank or investment accounts that will pass directly to them at the time of our death. Assets placed in a revocable trust naming them as beneficiaries will also pass directly, circumventing a surviving spouse and the delays of probate as well. In turn, heirs would do well to protect their inheritances from loss to a spouse's debts or a divorce.

Parents could also reduce uncertainties by transferring assets to their adult children even sooner if they can afford to. (But do not give away your property too early, warns the scribe Joshua ben Sirach in the second century BCE, "lest you change your mind and must ask for it back.")[142] Passing on assets *inter vivos* in fixed amounts as advances or even full inheritances while we live, rather than bequeathing amounts or shares *post mortem* (ours) or *post-post mortem* (at the death of a surviving spouse), can benefit all concerned. Earlier timing enables benefactors to take pleasure in the giving and to enjoy the recipients' pleasure as well, for example. It profits from the "time value" of money, given that it's worth more to beneficiaries now than it will be later. And it could relieve the tension inherent in heirs wondering how long a parent or stepparent will live while watching surreptitiously for signs of their (our?) demise.

True, there may be gift taxes to pay if annual transfers to children (or anyone else, the numbers of beneficiaries being unlimited) exceed $15,000 per recipient, beginning 2018, and twice that for married couples. But these taxes are not due at the time the gifts are made but at our death, and then only if the amount of our lifetime "excess giving"—when added to our estate—surpasses the total amount exempt from federal gift and estate tax.[143] Why, we might ask, should the prospect of estate taxes in the future inhibit us from doing what seems fair while we're alive?

Placing fixed assets in a trust to be turned over when children reach a certain age regardless of when we die is another option for reducing uncertainties and avoiding "the deathwatch." For the fictional Leonard Plumb Sr. in the quotation that opens this chapter, that would be forty years.[144] It could be sooner, though, or even later. "My father left money for me in trust," confides a friend in her forties. "But I can't collect until I'm *sixty*! What was he thinking?" He may have been thinking—quite reasonably—that his daughter could (should) provide for herself while she was working but that an infusion of cash would be welcome when she retires. The timing may seem odd but the certainty is reassuring.

As testators, some of us have a spouse but no children; some have children but no spouse; some have neither, but do have other family members or friends or caregivers whom we would like to "remember" in our wills. There are also contributions to good causes to make. How do we balance our moral obligations to our families and our communities at this point in our lives?

Perhaps the most powerful critique of inheritance practices in the United States is that family wealth piles upon wealth at the upper ends of the distribution. But it's not just wealth *per se* that matters; it's the power and privilege that go with it. "How does family wealth get transmitted to the next generations?" asks economist Fabian Pfeffer.[145] Most is transmitted relatively early in life, most powerfully through parental investments in education that augment children's future earning power. But being brought up in affluent neighborhoods with influential social networks and making "good" marriages, among other advantages, all play a role. Inheritance, says Pfeffer, is "the cherry on the top." Nevertheless, it can be a very big cherry indeed. Wealth on wealth tightens the link between money and opportunities for generations to come.

It would seem, then, that social justice could be served if—in addition to paying our fair share of estate taxes—the more fortunate among us were to take advantage of our testamentary freedom to distribute our largesse beyond the immediate family to benefit other people and organizations. And, indeed, "Testamentary freedom is highly correlated with the condition of sufficient assets," explain the authors of *The Family and Inheritance*.

> Individuals who are well-to-do usually have sufficient assets to take care of the natural objects of their bounty and also to give to others. Frequently, their spouses and children are not in

great need of their beneficence.... Well-to-do individuals are in the best position to meet their familial responsibilities and to a large degree fulfill community expectations...[146]

Key phrases in this passage offer a useful framework for thinking about the choices we make.

Sufficient assets. This is a relative term, of course: what is sufficient to one will not be to another. Still, it's possible that we're better off than we think we are. When everything is added up, most Americans have something of significance to leave behind.[147]

According to the U.S. Census Bureau, the median net worth of all households in 2011 with heads or single persons aged sixty-five to sixty-nine was $170,000.[148] Despite stark inequalities within this age group (the poorest 10 percent own less than $400 in net assets, the wealthiest 10 percent $900,000 or more), this is *two and one half times higher* than the median for all U.S. households. Net worth drops at age seventy-five on up, however. In large part this is because the proportion of men and (especially) women who live alone—and thus the percentage of households consisting of one person—shoots up fast at that age.[149] Married-couple households with heads age sixty-five and over report far higher combined net assets (median $285,000) than do men and women that age who live alone ($130,000 and $104,000, respectively).

To take care of the natural objects of our bounty. The "natural objects of our bounty" refer conventionally to our spouse and direct descendants—a very pared down version of the extended families of yore, and of many other parts of the world. What do they need, what can we give, and what is sufficient for their "care"? When John Stuart Mill proposed in the nineteenth century that only the spouse and minor children should have a right to inherit in intestacy cases, and then "only what they need to avoid being a burden on society" (the rest to be transferred to the public good), he was taking a particularly hard line. But the question of how much these "natural objects" really do need from us—as compared with what they might want, or would be happy to have, or feel entitled to—is a legitimate one. Does a spouse have the wherewithal to live in the manner to which she or he is accustomed without inheriting more? When is enough "enough" for our children, considering how much they may have received from us so far?

And also to give to others. Who else within or outside our immediate family circle might we include in our will or trust? "Partners, charities, siblings, nieces, nephews, and friends are all potential beneficiaries of your estate," writes Anne Warren in *Philanthropy and Wealth Planning*.[150] And there may be other needy and/or deserving persons in our lives: our partner's children, for example; sons- and daughters-in-law, the children of close friends; dedicated caregivers, kind neighbors, faithful employees and other "objects" of our affection, gratitude or concern.

And fulfill community expectations. This phrase applies more generally to our responsibility as society's members to contribute financially to the common good at our death as well as during our lifetimes. "Charities" is a rather old-fashioned name for what we're more likely to call nonprofit organizations. The designation covers an array of groups, foundations, and other institutions engaged in religious endeavors, the arts and humanities, education, science, environmental protection, medicine, social welfare, and other causes large and small. Contributions to registered charitable organizations and to family foundations set up for charitable purposes are tax-deductible, whether they are made during our lifetimes or at the time of our death.[151] One can also make contributions that are not tax-deductible to entities such as political parties or for-profit enterprises engaged in work that we value. One doesn't need to be a big-time philanthropist. Modest donations to projects such as such as a community Boys and Girls Club or a college scholarship fund can open up new opportunities in young people's lives.

Approximately 8 percent of Americans name charities in their estate plans. Wealthy testators tend to contribute larger shares of their assets to nonprofits—or to their own family foundations or to large public endowments such as hospital wings, university buildings or opera houses—than others do. Among people who died in 1995 with federal estate tax returns reporting at least $600,000 in gross assets (fewer than 4 percent of all decedents that year), testators with less than $1 million left an average of 18 percent of their estates to charity compared with 36 percent among those worth $10 million or more.[152]

Marital status and gender as well as wealth make a difference. Single women with estates of $600,000 or more in 1995 were more likely than single men in this wealth category to give to charity; widows more likely than widowers; and wives more likely than husbands. The average value of women's contributions is lower than men's, however ($588,000 vs. $888,000), reflecting their lower average net worth.[153] That so few husbands and wives make charitable bequests reflects their tendency to bequeath everything to their surviving spouse, whether or not the spouse is "in great need of their beneficence." Decedents of modest means, who are not included in this taxable estate sample, are far less likely to make charitable bequests, although they may well have contributed to their church and community organizations in other ways throughout their lifetimes.[154]

From a social justice and equity perspective, fairness would dictate that privately accumulated wealth should be partially redistributed through charitable giving and/or estate taxes when a person dies. One could, for example, leave a fixed amount to each of the named individuals and bequeath the remainder of the estate, whatever it may be, to the social good. But from the perspective of a surviving spouse or adult children, siphoning off money that "ought to be" theirs may seem highly unfair unless such sharing has been part of their upbringing and current way of life. Children's sense of fairness may also depend on the source of parental assets. If assets were mostly inherited from older generations, then the younger generation may feel a greater sense of entitlement to this "family money" than if the assets derived from parental income and investments, which could grant parents more freedom to bequeath assets to non-family members or to institutions or organizations.

This turns us back to the values of the will maker. With testamentary freedom, some parents may not feel obliged to support grown children after their own death if they have provided abundantly during the children's lifetimes. Indeed, estate planners sometimes advise wealthy parents not to leave "too much" to their children, directly or even in trust. If there is little to leave in any case, then a parent might simply say, "We did the best we could; the rest was up to you."

The decision is not always an easy one. "Daniel is making good money," explains a divorced mother recently retired from her profession. "And he'll get more when his father dies. Why should I feel guilty if I leave most of my money to other people and to political organizations? The pressure is pretty intense, though. After all, he's my son."

Nor does the decision end there. If the natural objects of our bounty include two or more adult children, how should each be treated? What about stepchildren? Should siblings inherit equally or unequally? Why, or why not? What principles of fairness arise when it comes to deciding among offspring with different needs and prospects, especially when some seem more deserving than others? We consider these questions in Chapter Four.

PART TWO

FAMILY CHOICES

CHAPTER FOUR

"To My Children I Leave..." When Equal Is Not Equitable (and Vice Versa)

Issues of fairness color most decisions in inheritance. Deciding what is fair, ...how to distribute assets among children who have experienced various degrees of success or failure, or whether there is any money to leave at all greatly challenge family ideologies.[155]

What seems fair to the parents may not be to the children.[156]

How should an estate be divided among grown children? Perhaps these are our own children, natural or adopted, now grown up. Perhaps we have stepchildren. Grandchildren too. Some may have lived with us when they were young, others not. Some may have moved away while others remain close. If we don't have children ourselves, we may consider those of a sibling or close friend as family and plan to give something to them.

But here's the problem. Even if they're all of the same genera-tion, they are likely to be at different places in their lives, with dif-ferent needs, prospects and resources. Some have kids of their own; others are still in college, perhaps with a student loan to pay off. A son is raking in the benefits of company stock options; a daughter is pregnant again, struggling as a single mom. She's refused help in the past; indeed, she's told us to get lost. What to do?

Once again, conflicting principles of fairness and justice convey dif-ferent messages about how to apportion shares of an estate among grown siblings. (The issue of minor children and their needs, including guard-ianship, is not considered here.) Do we want to give an *equal* amount or share to each, regardless of their individual circumstances? Or should we give them an unequal but *equitable* amount that compensates for their differences, i.e., what each of them *needs* and *deserves*, from our point of view? What's fair in general, and in particular family circumstances?

Fairness may not be everything from the testator's point of view of course. Other rationales may prevail: avoiding estate and gift taxes, say, or fulfilling special obligations; favoritism, a desire for control, self-interest, even dislike.[157] Motives may be benign or vindictive, hidden or freely aired. "Fair shmair!" says one woman when asked about disin-heriting her son. "It's my money, and it's what I want to do." With tes-tamentary freedom the possibilities are many, the implications fraught.

To my children I leave...This sounds simple enough. But whom do we count as our children? If we die intestate in the United States (and with no surviving spouse or other claimants that precede children in state statutes), our estate will be divided equally among our biological and adopted children. Whoever is our proven genetic offspring—whether the product of a long marriage or a casual encounter—is our child, and is equally entitled. A legally adopted child also counts equally in intestate cases. If a child dies before us, that child's share will fall *per stirpes* (within that branch of the family) to her or his children. Stepchildren as well as foster children are typically excluded, although state laws may make some exceptions (for example, if the deceased had declared his or her intention to adopt). Not only is there no genetic or legal connection with them, but it is also assumed that the natural parents of stepchildren—and of a surviving spouse of a deceased child of our own, for that matter—will provide for them.[158]

In intestacy it is the *genetic/biological/blood ties* and legal formalities (marriage, adoption, divorce) that determine who is family and who is not. But family forms are evolving fast. Marriage (conventional or same-sex), remarriage, or simply living together in domestic partnerships increasingly involves stepparenting and other arrangements such as assisted reproduction or sharing other people's children during their (and our) lives. When it comes to making our wills, our *social/relational/emotional ties* may reinforce the statutory rules or they may undermine them. Estrangement can sever the genetic ties, for example, particularly for a divorced father who lost custody and hasn't seen his children in years. At the same time, emotional attachment can override the lack of genetic connections, especially with regard to a new partner's children, whom we may have helped raise and who remain a significant part of our lives.

If we do not wish to include a biological or adopted child in our will, we must name the excluded child and make a specific declaration to that effect. Otherwise, she or he may file a claim against the estate on the grounds that we "forgot." By the same token, we must name the biological offspring we do wish to include. And if we are adding an adopted child, foster child or stepchild, then we must name that person too, and state the relationship.

All other things being equal (which they never are), should stepchildren be treated the same as offspring for whom we're accountable for their very existence? These are personal decisions, of course. Ethicists point out that there are many justifiable bases for treating people differently. "For example, we think it is *fair and just* when a parent gives his own children more attention and care...than he gives the children of others ..."[159] Moreover, legacies of family names and traditions, ancestors on family trees, and the continuity of bloodlines can carry great weight. For many parents who have both biological and stepchildren, the idea of favoring genetic offspring in inheritance decisions will seem both natural and right. For others, not so much.

A Pew Research survey conducted in 2010 found that one in five Americans age fifty and over has at least one stepchild.[160] When asked how obligated they would feel to provide assistance to family members who were dealing with a serious problem and needed either financial help or caregiving, 78 percent of respondents with both a grown biological child and a grown stepchild said they would feel "very obligated" to provide assistance to their natural child; 62 percent said they would feel "equally obligated" to their grown stepchild. Clearly, it's not simply a question for testators of inclusion or exclusion. Although stepchildren are not legally entitled to a share of the estate in cases of intestacy, attorneys may counsel a more nuanced approach:

> Do your stepchildren rely on you for support? What other resources do they have? If a stepchild has a realistic expectation of an inheritance from another parent or grandparent, that can be incorporated into your planning.... The closer the

relationship and the greater the need, the more likely it is that you'll want to provide for your stepchildren.[161]

What's interesting about this advice is that the same consideration could apply to our biological offspring. Should we treat them equally or unequally in our inheritance decisions? What if half-siblings have different expectations of inheritance from their other parent or grandparents?[162] Do factors such as closeness and need play a role? If so, how? What's fair, what's not, and why?

The most obvious rule of fairness is to give *to each equally* among siblings of the same generation and genetic relationship to us.[163] The principle here is that every child has an equal claim on their family's resources and on their parents' love and affection. It is one with which the overwhelming majority of will makers in the United States apparently agree:

> What the empirical evidence shows is that, in estate planning, most parents, regardless of ethnicity, think it is important to give each child an equal piece of the pie. They feel it is the *right thing to do*.[164]

Financial advisors, too, typically advise us to treat our children equally. "In my experience," writes the author of a *Wall Street Journal* opinion piece on "The Hazards of Unequal Inheritance," "it's never a good idea for clients to split their estate on an unequal percentage basis among children. It doesn't matter what the reasoning is, the children don't understand and they can become angry and resentful."[165]

In sum, both intestate statutes and our social norms favor equal bequests to siblings. But if this is so widely considered "the right thing to do," albeit with a few qualifications, then what do we make of arguments that take the opposite point of view?

More than two thousand years ago, Aristotle pronounced as the "most fundamental principle of justice" that "Equal people should be treated equally and unequal people unequally." Two hundred plus years ago, Thomas Jefferson—an avid reader of the Greeks—contributed his own version of this theme: "There is nothing more unequal than the equal treatment of unequal people." And in 2001, philosopher John Rawls in his book *Justice as Fairness* described several types of inequalities that should be rectified by applying the "difference principle."[166] In other words, if equal *outcomes* or *results* matter more to us than equal *treatment* or *opportunity*, and if *equitable* is more important than *equal*, then giving children equal shares of our estate is not the best way to go.

It is possible, of course, that our views about what's fair in family inheritance (as in society at large) are not swayed by concerns about equality of treatment *or* of outcome, as compared with, say, rewarding people for their productivity or punishing them for bad behavior. Why should principles of equality carry such weight? As modern-day ethicists remind us, there are numerous criteria for treating people differently in the name of justice and fairness, such as *need, desert, contribution, and effort,* quite apart from the closeness of our genetic or social ties.[167] Couldn't these criteria apply to what we bequeath our adult children as well?

Being fair to your children doesn't mean that you have to treat them all equally. Treat each child as an individual and think how best you can meet the needs of that child, while still taking care of your other beneficiaries.[168]

Some testators do treat their children unequally in their wills, and with good reason, at least in their view. One national study drew on a sample of women aged forty-five to eighty who had written their wills and had at least two children aged eighteen or older. "Will your estate be divided equally among your children?" they were asked.[169] Ninety-two percent said "yes," the rest "no." Mothers' intentions to bequeath unequal shares were not related to their family income, education, marital status or race. But, other things being equal, unequal intentions were significantly related to whether they had both biological and adopted or stepchildren; whether one child earned substantially more or less than the other(s); whether one or more children had kids but the other(s) did not; and whether the mother herself was in poor health, thus perhaps receiving or anticipating help from one of her children.

The survey asked women who answered "no" to explain why they planned to make unequal bequests. Summarized colloquially, virtually all of their reasons (except for one woman who declared "Nobody's business why") draw—whether wittingly or not—on one or more of the principles of fairness and justice reviewed below. Should we, for example, leave more to the sibling who has less, that is, *to each according to his or her need?* We explore this principle first.

If siblings who are now in their thirties, forties or fifties are all reasonably well off (or more than reasonably so), or, alternatively, if they are equally *not* well off and struggling to keep their heads above water, then questions of differential need will not arise. The principle of treating equal people equally would apply, quite apart from the size of the pie to be divided up among them. But if siblings are not equal in this sense, then the second part of this principle comes into play: treat unequal people unequally. That is, differential treatment is warranted, but it's ethical and fair from this point of view only if it benefits the least well off.

Mothers in the national survey just mentioned justified their intentions to give unequally in their wills with words such as "Oldest son has more assets than youngest son" and "Daughter will be living in house and needs it".[170] Economists who study different types of cash and in-kind transfers within families use concepts such as *compensatory justice* and *altruistic motives* to describe these behaviors, although respondents may not recognize themselves in these abstractions.

Whether we believe that we should compensate children with bequests that favor the worse off relative to the better off is likely to depend on how we perceive the nature, origins, and likely duration of their need, among other considerations. There are the "deserving needy" and the "undeserving needy." Whose fault *is* it if things turned out very differently for one sibling than for another, for example, and one is in dire straits while another is thriving?

The answers are sometimes clear. On the no-fault side, a child may have a physical or mental impairment that makes employment difficult or requires costly lifetime care. Or despite having reasonably equal opportunities in life, bad luck and misfortunate can intervene.[171] On the more fault-prone side, a child might have a serious drug dependency that may or may not respond to treatment. One daughter saves every penny that she can; another squanders everything that comes her way.

In cases such as these, parents might be advised to provide fairly for their children—if they can afford it—by setting up a managed irrevocable trust in which a trustee is charged with allocating funds at particular times for particular purposes or for paying certain expenses directly. Whether the children themselves view such limitations (eerily referred to as "dead hand controls") as fair is another question entirely, of course.

Quite apart from these extreme cases, children's financial needs can be volatile and uncertain as their life situations change for the better or worse. Estate planners warn that our attempts to anticipate future needs and even to respond to current ones by making specific bequests in our wills can miss the mark entirely.

We may also question whether giving additional money at our death is the best response to the need. Will it actually make a difference, and for how long? Moreover, differences among siblings in their current needs often result from decisions each of them has made in the past: continuing or dropping out of school, for example; marrying young or staying single; having no children or three or four; moving in and out of the labor force; choosing a low-paying occupation over a less satisfying but high-paying one; getting divorced, and so on. Is it, then, fair to reward with a larger bequest the child who made one set of family or career choices that didn't turn out so well, and to withhold from another because she or he is, by all counts, highly successful?

A clear case in point relates to adult siblings' marital and child-bearing decisions. Just as the number of *our* offspring affects how much each will receive from us, the number of children each of *our children* has—and whether they have an earning partner or not—affects both their need and their responsibilities.[172] Do we say to the daughter or son with more kids, "Too bad, you made your bed, now lie in it?" Or do we compensate for the differential need by, say, making gifts to the grandchildren directly while we're living or in our wills? Attorneys often recommend that grandparents who can afford it help out grandchildren directly with school expenses, summer camps, or other gifts and investments while sticking to the equality principle for their parents.

By and large, Americans agree that treating children unequally in their wills is *not* the answer, as we have seen. But this doesn't mean that parents don't respond to children's different needs during their lifetimes. They do. As we see next, they do so primarily by transferring cash or other benefits to each child (and grandchild) *inter vivos*— that is, during their own lifetimes—rather than *post mortem*. They do this in varying forms and for different reasons and at different times, when the need arises, while typically leaving the equal provisions of their wills intact.

Still, there are good reasons why we might wish to adjust our bequests to achieve a more equitable distribution of *what has already been given* relative to what we pass on at the time of our death. This assumes that we have kept some sort of reckoning of what each sibling has received of special value that the others have not. In intestate cases, the Uniform Probate Code states that property given to an heir during that individual's lifetime could be treated as an advancement against his or her intestate share only if the decedent declared or the heir acknowledged in writing that the gift was an advancement.[173] As testators we might want to consider this as a principle of fairness as well. Let's call it *balancing the scales of lifetime giving*.

The value of major cash or other gifts to adult children is difficult to track precisely. A parent may not recall them all, or know exactly what to count. What about a thirty-year-old son who lived at home rent-free for a few years to save money for a down payment on a condo, or a daughter who insisted on a luxurious "destination wedding"? Tuition costs, help with car or house payments, a tide-over loan that wasn't paid back, and outright cash gifts all count. Adding to the difficulties is the possibility that perspectives of the younger generation may differ from their parents' and even from one another as to which sibling received what, especially if some of the gifts were made quietly (e.g., a timely check in the mail).[174]

Helping young adult progeny to pay the rent is a common form of intergenerational transfer. One national survey found that 40 percent of twenty-two- to twenty-four-year-olds received some financial assistance from their parents for living expenses, averaging about $3,000 per year for those who got anything. According to the survey, living expenses account for only 20 percent of the help that parents eventually give to their adult children however. The bulk of the support comes in the form of lump-sum gifts for things like a down payment on a house or capital to start a business."[175]

If we count parental (and grandparental) support to offspring between the ages of eighteen to thirty, the value of transfers including housing, food, assistance with college, and cash soars to $50,000 on average, including those who received no such transfers.[176] Young adults in this 2015 survey whose parents are in the top quarter of income earners received transfers of $95,000 on average, those in the bottom quarter $31,000.

Estate planners encourage affluent clients to make yearly transfers to their children in order to reduce their estate tax liability. But for most parents, gifts to adult children tend not to be so systematic. Economists call these sporadic gifts "lumpy:" they occur now and then, in chunks, this year more to one person, next year more to another—or perhaps to the same one who is still (or once more) in need.

It is through these unequal lifetime transfers, *not* through unequal bequests, that most parents tend to give "to each according to his or her need." Overwhelmingly, it appears that *equal is fair when it comes to bequests; unequal is fair* (altruism, compensatory justice) *when it comes to helping children out when they need it.* Whereas only 8 percent of mothers in the national study said they intended to divide their estates unequally among their children, for example, 82 percent said they had made unequal gifts to them.[177] On a similar note, a national survey of asset and health dynamics among older adults found that only one-third of parents who gave any cash gifts to their adult children in the past year gave something to each one.[178] A child with an income below $20,000 was six times more likely to receive a cash gift than a sibling with an income of $50,000 or more, while poorer siblings were twelve times more likely to co-reside with a parent than richer siblings. Still, 90 percent of the parents' wills named all children as beneficiaries, and, of these, 95 percent provided "about equally" for each. The pattern is clear:

> Recent research on cash transfers...finds that parents give more gifts and larger gifts to their poorer children. Studies of bequests...in contrast, find that estates are most often divided in equal shares among children, regardless of their relative incomes.[179]

Is it surprising that older parents on the whole don't attempt a little compensatory justice in writing their wills? After all, this would help to balance the scales of earlier cash or in-kind transfers. Certainly there are examples of how this is done. Consider this provision in the will of president Richard M. Nixon:

> The specific bequests to my grandchildren named above are made to equalize the gifts made to all of my grandchildren during my life. The disparity in amounts, or lack of bequest, is not intended and should not be interpreted as a sign of favoritism for one grandchild over another.[180]

Although the bequests in question are to grandchildren, the principle is clear: the unequal amounts are specifically intended to offset lifetime gifts. Note the addendum, however: they are not to be interpreted as favoring one child over another. That would suggest a different principle: *to each according to his or her "just deserts."*

Among the definitions of fairness and justice is this: "Justice means giving each person what he or she deserves or, in more traditional terms, *giving each person his or her due.*[181] This neatly circular definition permits of several interpretations.

From a social justice or human rights perspective, for example, we could contend that everyone deserves to be treated equally, with dignity and respect. This, at the very least, is our due, along with the fulfillment of our basic human needs. In this context, each of us is owed equal treatment and perhaps equal results, equal happiness, equal wealth! The phrase "just deserts" serves as an apt warning, however. Are we really equally entitled? Or must we earn what we get, one way or another?

Shifting to a more judgmental interpretation, we could argue that each of us (including our children) should, indeed, get what we deserve, which may be a lot or not very much. Encompassing the extremes of reward and punishment, praise and blame, honor and shame, this perspective lends itself to a sort of Final Judgment in our Last Will and Testament. A child may be showered with gifts and blessings or disinherited in every sense, dishonored, and cast out from his or her people. Just deserts can become *retributive justice* in this interpretation, a harsh means of getting back at someone who has become estranged rather than making things right.

Retribution can be a powerful (and perhaps justifiable) motive, especially in cases of parental divorce. "I'm leaving everything to you," a father says to one of his daughters. "I haven't seen or heard from your sisters since your mother and I divorced. They always took her side." Or it can be less justifiable, as when a daughter or son is punished for marrying the wrong person, or disobeying a parental order, or not "making anything" of his or her life—or at least, a life as the parent envisioned it. With its implied or explicit enforcement mechanism involving the disinheritance of wayward family members, testamentary freedom clearly opens the door to such possibilities. As English philosopher Jeremy Bentham dryly remarked two centuries ago,

> The power of making a will encourages family virtue, represses vice, assures the testator against ingratitude, and generally keeps the family house in order.[182]

There is a middle ground in the interpretation of just deserts, however. Neither egalitarian nor punitive, economists refer to it as the principle of *reciprocity* or *exchange.* What does each of us "owe" to (and thus deserve from) one another in our social relations, especially between spouses and between parents and children?

The husband-wife nexus has seen fundamental transformations of the wife's social and economic subordination to an emphasis—if not always practiced—on equal rights and responsibilities. So, too, the parent-child relationship has shifted dramatically. For Aristotle, the obligation to serve and obey one's parents was an obligation to repay a debt. For theologian Thomas Aquinas, the commandment to honor one's parents meant providing a return for benefits received.[183] Today we tend to think far less of children's parental duties as compared with children's individual rights and parents' responsibilities to provide for their own retirement years. Still, parents expect to get *something* from their children. They (we) don't like to be ignored.

The principle of reciprocity is based on expectations that our adult progeny do owe us at least some warmth and attention, if not material help, in our later years in exchange for—and appreciation of—what we did for them when they were growing up. When this principle is violated, the reaction may run the gamut of anger, resentment, disappointment and hurt. "The expected behavior is implicit," observes one author, "and the failure to perform affects the parent in a direct and personal way."[184] A woman interviewed about her bequests explains, "Our daughter never comes to visit, and we don't see our grandchildren. What kind of thanks is that?" From the will maker's point of view the lack of reciprocity is unfair, a smaller inheritance or even none at all is fair.

The other side of just deserts is the reward for special help and affection when expectations of reciprocity are not just met but exceeded. "I'm giving the house to my youngest son and his wife," says one woman. "They've been wonderful. I don't know what I'd do without them." Older mothers in the national survey cited earlier mention several "exchange" reasons for making unequal bequests to their children. "We've gotten more from two children than from the third," says one.[185] Moreover, those who report their health as "fair" or "poor" are more likely to be receiving assistance from at least one of their children (one-third do so); more likely to have an adult child living with them (one-quarter); and more likely to say they will be giving unequal amounts to their children.[186]

Caring for an elderly parent can be contentious, however. On the one hand, a parent or the entire family may expect or even demand it, particularly in ethnic communities where such care is still very much the norm. On the other hand, a son or daughter may volunteer to do it, out of love and affection, duty, ability and proximity, or family tradition. According to a Pew Research survey, one in four adults aged forty-five to sixty-four in the U.S. is providing some type of unpaid care for an aging adult, usually a parent.[187] Siblings may be grateful that one of them has stepped in, thus relieving them of their own obligations (and guilt). Or they may become alarmed, concerned that one of them is "insinuating" himself or herself into the parent's life and affections, taking advantage of a parent's needs and vulnerability, perhaps using their presence to influence the parent's will.

Whereas a testator may wish to reward or compensate a caregiving child with a larger share of the pie, estate planners often advise against it because it could elicit resentment or even legal challenges from the remaining sibs. Instead, advisers are likely to recommend that a parent pay a caregiving son or daughter directly for services rendered or income foregone, where possible, while leaving the will intact.

This advice corresponds with the general observation that children who spend more time with their aging mothers and fathers tend to receive greater financial support from their parents *before* they die, which could be interpreted as reciprocity, exchange, or simple thanks.[188] But where this doesn't happen, siblings may well define an equal distribution of the parental estate as highly unfair in families where some have rendered multiple services and others, none.

Providing financial or other services to an aging parent represents one type of potentially unequal cost and responsibility that an adult sibling may incur. But there is another: a parent may, in a will, bequeath a business or property to a sibling who is expected, unlike the others (or perhaps in collaboration with them) to assume the primary responsibility for managing it. This principle of fairness involves giving *to each according to the responsibility incurred*.

I n England, passing on large estates to the first-born son conveyed not only privilege but also responsibility. As we saw in Downton Abbey, the heir—whether he wished it or not—was expected to manage the estate with its farm tenants, artisanal workers, domestic employees, family members, and various hangers-on. He was expected to fulfill the duties of the aristocratic title; support local village institutions; marry well and produce heirs; provide marriage portions for his sisters and income or settlements for his younger brothers, and much more.

Not all heirs fulfilled these expectations, of course, nor did they want to. Nor did non-inheriting family members necessarily think the system was fair, especially if they were sent off to make their own way in life. But it could be argued that the tradeoff was fair, even if the class system was not: property went to those who assumed the responsibility for it and who *used* it, and by custom this was the oldest son.

Detached from the link to primogeniture, similar arguments can be made today for passing on a family farm to the son or daughter who is willing (and knows how) to work it, a family business to the one who is willing (and knows how) to run it, a real estate "empire" (large or small) to the one who is willing (and knows how) to manage it. Indeed, it is not unusual for such transfers to be made in stages as the parent/owner turns over responsibilities (and perhaps even title) to the next generation and retires from an active role. "We're going to form this corporation, Ginny, and you girls are all going to have shares" announces the aging patriarch of Jane Smiley's novel *A Thousand Acres*. "You girls and Ty and Pete and Frank are going to run the show. You'll each have a third part in the corporation. What do you think?"[189]

The key words here are *willing* and *able*. And the question is, if the chosen heir(s) agree to do this, will the other siblings agree to settle for less?

On the other hand, when siblings are expected to *share* the ownership and control of indivisible assets such as a farm, a primary residence or summer home, or a family business, a fair settlement—that is, one that is acceptable to all—may be almost impossible to achieve. Personalities may conflict, needs and interests differ, and the availability (or lack of) time and other resources pull siblings in opposite directions.

In his book *Bargaining with the Devil*, Robert Mnookin describes a mediation involving three siblings who have inherited a valuable Cape Cod family vacation home as tenants in common. But the bequest carries major responsibilities that not all can assume (or want). Says one daughter, "Audrey":

> I live in Oakland, California, and I don't make a lot of money....
> The last thing in the world I need is a one-third interest in a waterfront estate three thousand miles away. I can't afford to pay my share of the annual upkeep and taxes, and now that both of our parents are gone, I'd never use the place.[190]

Audrey wants out, which means her two siblings must either buy her out (they can't afford to) or else sell the property (they're not willing to: they want to spend time there and pass it on to *their* children.) As it turns out, Mnookin negotiates an agreement that satisfies everyone (spoiler: a sale of part of the property, not including the main house), but not without threats of lawsuits and family split-ups hanging over everyone's heads.

Attorneys and estate planners have a lot to say on this topic. They strongly advise us to have "The Conversation" with grown children or other heirs about assets, inheritances, and the responsibilities they may incur in managing properties, a family foundation or a business. At the very least, our beneficiaries will be forewarned and have an opportunity tell us (and one another) whether the plans we are making—presumably for their benefit—are something they can manage, work with, or even want.

T estators may be guided by other norms of fairness in addition to those mentioned above, of course. "This is the way it's always been done with us" is one example. In other words, *to each according to what is customary.*

In his description of ethnicity, national origins and the treatment of heirs in the United States, sociologist Remi Clignet observes that the social norms that guide people of different cultural groups in the distribution of assets among their children—both during their lifetimes and at their death—distinguish in different ways among not only the value and function of the assets themselves, but also the birth order and gender of eligible heirs and their respective needs, capabilities and responsibilities.[191] Daughters in Muslim law inherit half of their brother's shares, for example, and stepchildren, illegitimate children and adopted children do not inherit. Muslims living in the United States may follow these religious prescriptions if they wish to do so simply by exercising their testamentary freedom. So, too, can people with traditions based on any one of a multiplicity of African, Asian, Latin American or European laws and customs.

Cultures also differ according to the shared rationales they invoke for rewarding or for punishing a particular heir, Clignet adds. "Favorite sons" and "dutiful daughters" play important roles in some traditions, as do ideas about the significance of bloodlines (male, female or both?); family honor (threatened by sexual transgressions?); legitimacy and illegitimacy (do children born out of wedlock have rights?); and marital and filial obligations (who owes obedience to whom?).

The principle of giving to each according to custom can result in highly unequal allocations of family assets to descendants based on birth order, gender, and other preferences. Such differential treatment may be justified on the grounds that the norms *are known to and shared by* all members of a group or community. To the extent that no one is singled out and that everyone lives in anticipation of them, the argument goes, then customary practices could be considered "fair." As attorney Mark Accettura remarks,

The customs, mores, and laws of the day define societal and individual inheritance expectations and provide a standard from which fairness can be measured.... Fairness, of course, is subjective. Rules, no matter how generous or restrictive, are measured by whether they are applied evenly.[192]

The principle of custom is invoked not only to describe the ethnic "other," however, but also to what Clignet refers to as "the dominant

American practice of dividing shares equally among heirs."[193] It is *customary to do so,* just as it is customary *not* to include our adult children's spouses in our bequests even though they are family members and parents of our grandchildren as well. Nor, as we have seen, is it customary to include our stepchildren in bequests, although we may make exceptions.

This brings us back to the question, What is family? As will makers with testamentary freedom, we can include or exclude whomever we like, even from among our own children. And, once we delineate who is included and excluded, we can treat siblings of the same generation equally or unequally, depending on numerous societal and individual factors. The decisions we make may be based on one or more of the principles of fairness and justice reviewed here, or they may not.

"In my experience," writes California attorney Ivette Santaella, "parents do not give it much thought about how to apportion their estate; they automatically decide to leave their assets equally to all of their children. It is very rare that I have a parent or parents come in having thought out the equity of leaving more assets to one child [than another]..."[194]

What happens when equal is not equitable among siblings, or vice versa, from *their* point of view? How are they likely to react? And what happens when siblings are faced with the prospect of settling the estate and dividing up a parent's personal belongings and the contents of what may have been a family home filled with childhood memories? Much depends on who has been given the responsibility. "The real concern parents have," Santaella continues, "is not who is going to get the money, but who will control the assets—i.e., who will be the trustee or executor. In these situations I encourage them to have a family meeting, because nine times out of ten, I have seen this end up in families breaking apart."

The role of the executor(s) or trustee(s) responsible for implementing the terms of the will or trust is discussed in the next chapter. How does this work? Is the process a fair one from the beneficiaries' point of view? The perspective shifts too, from that of testator-parents preparing an estate plan to that of adult siblings (full, half, or step) deciding among themselves what is a fair "division of the spoils" after a parent's death. Complications loom. Can family harmony be maintained? As we shall see, the siblings' decision-making process elicits one more principle of fairness: *to each according to what is jointly agreed.* How might *this* work?

CHAPTER FIVE

FROM OUR PARENTS WE RECEIVE: THE DIVISION OF THE SPOILS

Although personal possessions may have financial as well a sentimental value, it is the impossibility of dividing personal property with sentimental value in a way considered fair to all involved that presents challenges. Different perceptions among siblings, older parents, estate executors, and other family members of what "fair" means...quickly emerge...[195]

I f as a parent we were to write the most basic of wills, we might include a clause (perhaps prefaced, if we're married, by "If my spouse does not survive me...") that goes something like this: "I give my [tangible personal] property to those of my children who survive me, in equal shares, to be divided among them by my executors in their absolute discretion after consultation with my children."[196]

Some of us might wish to embellish our Last Will and Testament with gifts to friends, family members and others: an antique Persian carpet, say, or a collection of stamps or coins, or the grandfather clock. Benjamin Franklin made certain in his 1788 will that his daughter,

Sarah Bache, would receive "The king of France's picture, set with four hundred and eight diamonds."[197] Thomas Jefferson willed to his grandson in 1826 "my silver watch in preference of the golden one, because of its superior excellence, my papers of business...as my executor, [and] all others of a literary or other character...as of his own property."[198]

Gifting personal items in a will or referenced memorandum will certainly make one's intentions clear. But testators often begin distributing things well before (or in anticipation of) their death. Intentions are clear here too, but siblings and other potential claimants may worry that it's not fair because things are "disappearing," a parent is playing "favorites," or someone else has "got there first."

And here's the dilemma: we are free to give our personal possessions to whomever we wish while we live, and to leave them to whomever we wish at our death. Legally, our progeny are not entitled to anything unless we die without a will. Yet, chances are that they will *feel* entitled, in different ways and to different things. And chances are that they will find something unfair about the process by which a parent starts giving (or throwing) things away in later life, as well as in the process by which they undertake their *post mortem* "division of the spoils."

We are not talking here about titled property such as bank accounts, corporate shares, real estate, or other major items covered by a will.[199] Rather, we're talking about what is variously described as "untitled property," "tangible personal property," or, more popularly, as the remainder of an estate (as in "Estate Sale"), our "stuff" or our "things." These may be items of substantial value or they may be everyday items such as furniture, kitchenware, books, photo albums and clothing. If we move or get a divorce, we pack them up and take them with us. When we die, they're left behind.

What happens to our personal things? In this chapter we consider how heirs decide to apportion among themselves the "residue" of the estate. What principles of fairness will they bring to bear, explicitly or implicitly, in their claims of who should get what? But first let's consider the role of a principal actor in this drama: the executor or trustee. What is she or he supposed to do, and with what authority?

A will must name an executor to be valid; a revocable trust must have a successor trustee. (If we die intestate, the courts appoint a personal representative.) But who will this be? The job is an onerous one that can extend for months or even for years in probate if the estate is a complicated one, or if the will is contested.

The executor is responsible for identifying and protecting everything the decedent owned until all decisions have been made about what, when and how property will be liquidated and distributed. Also, for collecting, inventorying and valuing the assets of the estate; conforming to state laws; paying bills (attorney's fees, court fees, accountants, capital gains taxes, debts, funeral expenses); representing the estate in claims if there is litigation; and preparing financial reports. Only when all that (and more) has been done can the property left in the will be transferred to the heirs.[200]

As the personal representative of the deceased, the executor is, above all, responsible for carrying out her or his wishes to the letter— if such "letter" exists, that is. The executor is not to be sidetracked or dissuaded by the expectations or demands of heirs or would-be heirs. An executor who is also an heir, however—whether a surviving spouse or a daughter or son of the deceased—will be in a sticky situation if the other heirs charge a conflict of interest. It can be a thankless task.

Some estate planners contend that a surviving wife or husband should be both executor and sole beneficiary. This leaves the children out of the picture entirely, unless the spouse is willing to pass on some personal possessions of the departed, or gifts of cash. If the decedent does leave some share of his or her estate to the children directly, it is the executor-spouse—whether a natural parent or a stepparent to the heir-siblings—who makes the decisions, for better or worse.

If there is no surviving spouse and one of the inheriting siblings is appointed, who should it be? The oldest? The one who lives closest? The best educated? The most responsible? How will the other siblings react to the appointment? Relief? Resentment? Both? Tensions can heighten when heirs learn that, legally, they are not entitled to see the will until it has been filed in probate court, although trusts are a different matter. "My parents chose as co-executors the two among the five of us who were closest to them geographically and who had professional legal training," one woman explains. "They didn't think about how old sibling rivalries and lack of connection might affect us, or about the conflict of interests, real or perceived. My trust in the situation was broken when I realized I wasn't being informed about what was going on. Was it personal, or because I lived across the country? I hired a lawyer to help me understand the process and make sure I got the advice I needed."

For all of these reasons and more, some estate planners recommend that testators with a relatively modest estate appoint a reliable friend or other relative (brother-in-law, niece, etc.) with the backup of professional assistance, especially in blended families:

Assign a trusted family member or friend to serve as the executor of your estate. It is usually not wise to appoint as executor one of the children who will gain from the distribution of your possessions.[201]

For larger estates, professional fiduciaries are recommended, perhaps with assistance from a family member. The hired executor or trustee might work independently or with a bank, trust company, or accounting or law firm. The downside of this option, of course, is that it will cost.

One of the more prickly assignments that executors take on is overseeing the disposition of the decedent's personal belongings. In some families the process plays out in an orderly fashion with mutual consideration and convenience (or indifference) all around. In others, it's a feeding frenzy.

Assessing the financial and sentimental value of the assembled belongings is crucial, no matter how large or how small the estate may be. But so, too, are the emotions that siblings bring with them. And unless the parent has made gifts of personal possessions explicit, what is left behind is quite literally up for grabs. A surviving spouse may be pitted against the grown children and *their* partners and children and vice versa. Ideally, an executor will impose calm and reason on this process.

Some estate attorneys advise testators not leave their separate personal property to a surviving spouse if he or she is not the biological parent of the surviving siblings unless it is intended as a specific gift, in which case it should be in writing. If property is to pass to the spouse for his or her use and enjoyment, then the testator is advised to leave written instructions about which possessions should go to the children by a certain date, or when the survivor moves, remarries, or dies. Otherwise, items may be given to step children, sold, lost or tossed, the new owner unaware of or indifferent to the value they may have to the children of the deceased.

This advice applies to property left in wills as well. Estate litigators interviewed in four American cities report that, aside from legal challenges based on testamentary capacity or undue influence, it is changes in family structure and divorce and remarriage that elicit the most litigation in their practices.[202] In a typical scenario, the offspring of a first marriage of a deceased father challenge a subsequent wife for larger shares of the estate or the family home—or vice versa.

Whether there is a surviving spouse or not, family heirlooms, household goods and personal effects might well be distributed at least partially while one or both of the parents is still alive, especially if they move from a house into a condo, apartment, retirement community or assisted living. Often, however, the major division occurs quite soon after the second parent's death. It may be when the family gathers for a funeral or memorial service. Or it may extend over months, depending on where adult siblings live and what complications arise. Typically it will happen while the will is in probate or the trust is being settled. There will be a lot going on, and it's likely to be demanding.

The executor or successor trustee is legally in charge of all of these proceedings. This is where the question of who has been designated for the task becomes highly relevant. If it's a professional, he or she may rely on family members for advice and may even turn over the division of personal possessions entirely to them. If it's a family member, tensions may well arise as to the authority this person assumes over other family members and the timing and nature of the decisions being made.

Heirs may disagree about whether to keep or sell a house or other real estate, for example, whether to keep or sell shares of stocks, how to equalize the distribution of assets in the will, what to do with a family business. There may be unpleasant surprises in the will itself. Heirs may demand immediate satisfaction of their claims, unwilling to wait until all is settled. Amidst all this and the mounting costs of funerals and memorial services and travel and attorneys' and accountants' fees and other administrative expenses, executors and heirs must devise a method for dividing up the belongings a parent (or aunt or uncle or grandparent) has left behind. How is this done? Do rules exist to guide the process? Can we rise to the occasion in our own families?

The idea of negotiating an agreement about how to allocate "society's resources" draws on the premises of philosophers who contend that, as rational individuals, we can rise above our self-interests and adopt a set of guiding principles to ensure the common good, or, in this case, the good of the family members and others involved. As a practical matter, however, we can think of a number of qualifications to this optimistic premise when considered in the context of what may be quite contentious family matters. Moreover, unless a skilled facilitator organizes the negotiation process in a manner that gives everyone an equal voice, it is likely that family hierarchies will endure: the meek may end up with little and the powerful prevail.

As beneficiaries of a parent's estate, we may not be inclined to approach the task rationally despite our assertions to the contrary. The process could run fairly smoothly if one or more of the heirs expresses little interest in how things turn out, especially if they don't particularly want any of the goods on offer or live too far away. "I'll just take a couple of small things," a sibling might say, "and you can do whatever you want with the rest." But the stories we hear, and our own experiences, are likely to be more complicated than that. Old grievances and personal slights may well emerge to color our perceptions of what's fair, what's not, and why. Some of them still hurt.

It's likely that every one of us has memories from our childhood of being treated unfairly. We were blamed for something we didn't do, or didn't mean to do, or that was an "accident." A sibling received praise we yearned for, or a coveted gift, or special treatment. We were made to share a favorite toy with a little brother who had his own toys, to do chores when others were playing, to obey without question. We compared what we were given, or what we were made or allowed to do, with what our siblings and friends were given, or were made or allowed to do. When we didn't get what we wanted or expected or felt we deserved, we shouted (or whined) *"Not fair!"*

Rules of fairness imbed themselves early in our psyches, nurtured by lessons learned and grievances endured. We become skilled in articulating these rules, adapting them to particular situations. As we grow older we elaborate and apply our own interpretation of these rules to our relationships with our families, friends and partners, and in our workplaces, communities, and society as a whole.

The death of a parent marks a critical passage in our lives. It signifies not only the mortality of a person upon whom we once relied, but also our own vulnerability. It is almost always a shock, even if it was expected. And it is almost always intensely emotional, even in ways that are unexpected. It is a time when families come together and a time when families may split apart. For perhaps no situation is so fraught as that in which family relationships are tested by our views of what's fair and what's not in the division of personal property belonging to a parent who died.

The financial value of titled property passed on in a will is likely to far exceed that of the things left behind. But research has shown that transfers of personal property elicit more contesting behavior from family members. Why is this?

For one thing, decisions no longer rest with the testator but with the recipients, grown children with a complex history of relationships with the deceased parent(s) and with one another. For another, as social scientist Marlene Stum points out in her research on family decision-making around inheritance issues, it's not just the emotions of the siblings themselves that come into play, but also the objects, and the meanings they invoke.

> Decisions about non-titled personal property involve dealing with the emotions and sentimental value connected to objects accumulated over a lifetime and across generations of family members.[203]

Unless heirs agree at the outset on how they are going to proceed, claims and counterclaims over particular objects can be personalized, insistent, and chaotic. *I want it. I need it. I can use it. I deserve it. I was promised it. I gave it to him. She would want me to have it. I was closer to him than you were. I appreciate it more than you do. You always get what you want. It's my turn. My kids can use it. You already have a lot of stuff. It will look better in my house. You'll only ruin it.* Each of these claims invokes a principle of what's just or fair in the circumstance. And as is typically the case, each can elicit an equally principled counter claim.

In the introduction to his book *The Idea of Justice*, economist Amartya Sen tells a story of three children arguing over who should keep a flute they have found.[204] One made it. One can play it beautifully. One doesn't have any other toys. Sen explains that the solution of who should keep it depends on our particular philosophy of justice (e.g., property to the producer, to the user, to the needy, although he uses different terms). It's simply not possible to settle the dispute in a universally accepted "just manner."

Coping with these competing claims of what's fair according to abstract principles of justice should be enough for us to deal with. But here is another perspective. Feminist critics assert that the justice perspective articulated by philosophers such as John Locke, Emmanuel Kant and John Rawls, which they call "an ideology of the dominant class," does not reflect the realities of women's position in society and the family. Nor does it reflect how women tend to draw on quite different considerations than men do when it comes to resolving ethical dilemmas such as deciding how to distribute the personal possessions of a deceased parent.

Philosopher Martha Nussbaum criticizes Rawls' principles of justice for not allowing for flexibility, for "*the willingness to give love and understanding priority over rigid norms,*" or—for that matter—for simply "being nice."[205] And in earlier work, psychologist Carol Gilligan, the author of *In a Different Voice,* draws on research into how women and men resolve moral choices in their lives and the reasoning they use. Distinguishing between the formal justice perspective and what she calls the *care perspective,* Gilligan demonstrates that women are more likely to consider matters such as attachment, understanding, being heard, and taking the feelings of others into account in deciding what's fair in particular circumstances.

> In place of the hierarchical ordering of values characteristic of the justice perspective, Gilligan's female respondents describe a network of connection, *a web of relationships* that is sustained by a process of communication.... For these women, moral problems do not result from a conflict of rights to be adjudicated by a ranking of values.... Rather, [they are]

imbedded in a contextual frame that eludes abstract, deductive reasoning.[206]

This is not to say that caring does not enter into the justice perspective. But, Gilligan argues, making exceptions to the rules for reasons of personal connection or affection leaves the hierarchical structure of the rules intact.[207]

In this feminist formulation of ethical decision-making, then, rationality (as in "what reasonable men transcending their self-interest agree to") isn't everything, nor is it even the most compelling thing. Emotions such as love, empathy, and feelings of personal responsibility nurture a more cooperative process of problem solving that takes contextual stories into account.

Of course some emotions—even positive ones of love and empathy—can get in the way of solving practical problems such as how to distribute valued personal possessions among siblings, especially if these concerns aren't shared by others. But so can uncompromising assertions of what's *right* that are based on "universal" principles of justice, each claiming to be rational from an ideological point of view.

What do we know of how siblings and other family members actually *do* make decisions in these circumstances? Anecdotal examples abound, but it's difficult to know what to make of them. Are they bizarre or typical? What *rules* did they use? Fortunately we can refer to one study that throws light on the process.

In her aptly titled investigation, "I Just Want to be Fair," family researcher Marlene Stum surveyed 64 older adults (55 females and 9 males) living in rural Midwestern communities about their individual perspectives as an adult participating with siblings in settling personal property inheritances from parents or parents-in-law.

That women made up most of the sample—reportedly a deliberate research decision, given women's greater interest in the topic—may well influence the responses to Stum's questions. When asked to describe their goals in the process, for example, her respondents emphasized three themes, at least two of which Gilligan would call "caring:" preserving and passing on family history and memories; keeping peace among family members by avoiding hurt feelings; and "being fair to all involved." But, Stum asks, what did they mean by "being fair"? "While each person had his or her own perception of what 'fair' meant," she writes, "each individual talked as if the meaning of 'fair' would be the same for everyone else."[208] This theme will be familiar from the previous chapter, with "sentiment" adding another layer of complexity:

> Rules for allocating personal property described by family members revolved around whether 'fair' meant being equal or being equitable and *which rules would apply to what possessions*.... The challenges involved in getting equal value when items may have a combination of financial and/or emotional value...were reflected in distribution methods used by families.[209]

In some families, "fair" meant that everyone received an equal number of items. In others, fair meant receiving items of equal emotional value, with siblings choosing a certain number of objects that were most meaningful to them. Some families attempted to put a financial value on all items so that siblings received equal financial value. Others auctioned them with play money.

Families choosing the equitable option were more likely to take individual differences into account when distributing resources. Siblings allocated their parent's possessions based on factors such as what each had contributed to the parent's financial, social, emotional and/or physical care; the relative financial, physical and emotional needs of the siblings themselves; and other personal characteristics. Birth order, current age, gender, marital status, and geographical location were taken into account in some families in determining who received what and how much, although a few participants perceived these criteria as unfair.

Respondents were also asked how family members decided on a method for making the distributions, that is, the "rules about rules." Stum calls this *procedural justice*, as distinct from the *distributive justice* of who gets what in the end.

The key assumption here, and one that is supported by other research, is that most of us are more prone to accept an undesirable outcome if we believe that the *process* was fair. But here again, individuals' perceptions don't necessarily coincide. This is because our individual judgment often depends on whether we get what we want or feel *we* deserve—that is, on the outcome—which in turn colors what we say about fairness of the process. A perfect circle, in other words.

Some survey respondents stressed the importance of having the *owner* (i.e., parent) make decisions about who should get particular items before he or she dies, preferably in writing, and preferably after offering all of the siblings an opportunity to choose. But this may not happen. And even if it does, decisions will almost always have to made about some personal possessions after the owner dies.

This is where procedural rules come into question. Who should decide on the rules? Siblings only? Everyone, including siblings' partners and *their* children (that is, daughters or sons-in-law and grandchildren)? Long-time caregivers? Opinions ran the gamut. In addition, timing, notification, inventories, valuation of items, methods by which participants chose, how to treat absent siblings, appeals after the fact, and other concerns all played a role in respondents' perceptions.

Underlying people's expressed concerns is an implicit framework for judging the fairness of a *process*. Drawing on examples from her respondents, Stum identifies five "internal guidelines" for making such a judgment: truthfulness, accuracy and full disclosure; avoidance of domination by more vocal, powerful or "entitled" siblings; consistency of implementation; ethical behavior (no pilfering); and who was and should be represented in the decisions and final distribution.

Professional estate settlers have plenty to say about the final distribution process. Opinions differ about some aspects. But all admonish us that everyone involved is expected to take responsibility for making things work smoothly.

As for testators, experts advise us as parents and grandparents to start giving things to our children and other favorites *now* or selling or donating them to good causes once our offsprings' (and our spouse's or partner's) wishes are known. If we intend to keep everything until the very last, then we should ask our heirs to choose a few things that they especially want for themselves after we die. If such gifts are to count toward the final distribution, they should be in writing with a declaration to that effect that includes dates, recipients, and approximate value.

Executors and trustees have multiple responsibilities too. In addition to those listed above, they are expected to protect all of the tangible personal property and prepare it for distribution, making sure to carry out the intent of the deceased. Property will need to be inventoried and a professional appraiser brought in, where necessary, to estimate the monetary value of collectibles, vintage and antique items. Executors may also oversee the final distribution.

As for the heirs, they (we?) are expected to be cooperative, mutually respectful, and fair. And they are expected to honor their parent's wishes as vested in the appointed fiduciary, whether family member or professional. Speaking rather sternly, personal property manager and "Estate Lady" Julie Hall insists that heirs or would-be heirs are entitled to receive *nothing* unless it was given to them by the testator or is approved by the executor. [210]

Almost everyone who has gone through the experience of settling an estate has a story to tell about someone else's bad behavior, along with advice about what and what not to do. Estate settlement books such as Hall's warn us of dubious types such as "the grief-stricken heir," "the guilt-ridden heir," "the hoarder heir," "the unscrupulous heir (thief)," "the greedy heir," "the entitled heir," "the feeling-slighted heir," and even "the 'do-gooder' heir." All may subvert a fair process by subtle or not-so-subtle means, insist on their special rights, or make a scene.

And now for the process itself. Ideally, the heir-siblings or their representatives (and perhaps others, such as a facilitator) will gather together or participate via proxy. To avoid major meltdowns, estate handlers advise us to do the following:

First, decide *beforehand* who is to have a say in the distribution. Most experts suggest limiting decisions to the heir-siblings themselves. Although Marlene Strum's survey respondents differed in their opinions about whether "fair" means siblings only or more inclusive representation, advisor Julie Hall is strict about this. "*Don't* include in-laws in the division process," she says. "Siblings come first and in-laws [and grandchildren, she adds] should stay out of it."[211]

Second, settle on goals and protocols. What are the priorities? Passing on a family heritage and preserving memories? Maintaining good relations? Protecting special collections intact within the family? Ensuring that everyone receives an equal number of things, or of equal monetary value, or of special personal significance to each? Is equal "equitable" in this particular situation?

Third, establish a selection technique depending on how these questions are answered. One simple method is to have everyone select one item in turn, beginning with a random start (high card?) and continuing until everyone has selected a fixed number of items. Then invite others to choose, such as grandchildren, other relatives, close friends, caregivers or neighbors. Donate or sell everything that's left.

A more formal procedure is to sort everything into categories, perhaps with a professional organizer. Classify valuable items such as heirlooms, antiques, paintings, silver, china, and collections of various kinds into categories of assessed or approximate monetary value. Then add groups of items with sentimental value (to some if not all) and possible use value (such as appliances, furniture, bedding, clothing, kitchen items). Take turns choosing from each category.

Striking a balance of monetary and sentimental value can be challenging when siblings differ in their tastes, preferences and priorities. Once again, Hall's advice is stern. "The *only methods that I recommend*," she says, require knowing the monetary values first and making sure that each heir receives an equivalent amount. How? "Heirs can purchase items based on appraised values...and the money collected is then split evenly."[212]

Note that monetary value trumps sentimental value in this approach. There's no talk here of using play money for auctions to the highest bidder until each person's stash is gone, or of setting prices at a fraction of their assessed worth. And although the total value for each heir is "equivalent" in the end, well-off siblings can more easily afford to buy the family heirlooms they'd like to keep than can their sisters and brothers who need cash for living expenses. What's fair about that?

Trust and estate planner Paula Leibovitz Goodwin has a different take on this process that focuses on family harmony rather than monetary value. She and her five siblings agreed to distribute their parents' personal property this way:[213]

"*The rules*: First, no one was allowed to go into the house until we all went in together (except for me as trustee/executor). Second, at the time of division, our spouses and children could not be there. (Important rule I think. Spouses can throw things off.) Third, I brought someone in who charged us hourly to let us know in a general way what items had more value than others. Fourth, if you gave the item to mom and dad, it was automatically yours."

"*The process*: In Round One, everyone had two or three hours to go around the house and look at everything. Each of us made a list of our top ten items in order of preference. We then went through everyone's first choice, second choice, etc. Often items were duplicated but they never ended up as the same number, so the higher preference got it. Round Two applied to items not picked in Round One. Everyone had another three hours to go around the house and post a colored sticker on an item they wanted. We decided multiple posts by a coin toss or straws. Items still left over were given to grandchildren and charities. I have two alpha sisters and it was a challenge but it worked out brilliantly," says Goodwin. "I have used this approach successfully with other families."

Other protocols may be acceptable depending on the size and nature of the estate and siblings' physical and emotional closeness, among other considerations. Some may be happy to give up their share because they really don't want or need anything from their parent's household. "I took few things of my mother's, some jewelry, nothing much. I live in a small apartment. My sister and her husband have four children so I told her to take everything else. It seemed fair at the time. It still does." Factors other than the formal rules may also come into play, such as Gilligan's care perspective. Says one woman in Stum's survey, "There were a few times when one member let another have an item even if he/she wanted it—just so there would be no hard feelings lingering later."[214]

In sum, fairness is clearly principled, but it's also contextual, fluid and responsive. It inheres in the process as well as the outcome. We all say that we "just want to be fair," but research shows that each of us is likely to have very different ideas about what fairness *is*—in general and as applied to a particular situation—even as we assume that others share our own perceptions. Indeed, it appears that, like beauty, fairness is in the eye of the beholder. This is particularly the case when the debate is not just about money but about objects of sentimental value, memories, favoritism, responsibilities, love, jealousy and other currencies of family life.

"The goal with my family and the goal of many of my clients is to have their children maintain their family connection when the parent is no longer in the picture," Goodwin explains. "As an attorney, at the time of death I like to bring all of the children of the deceased together and advise them that the greatest gift they were given is their family, and to remember this if they start to get mad about something. Is it worth losing a sibling over?"

This is an excellent question. Rather than (or in addition to) talking to survivors at the time of a death, however, what about bringing everyone together as participants in the estate planning process while the parent-testator is still alive? Is it possible in informal conversations or more formal mediated sessions to negotiate a general agreement about what's fair rather than risking hurt feelings, family breakup and costly litigation after the fact? How might this be done? We address these questions in the final chapter.

CHAPTER SIX

CAN FAIRNESS BE NEGOTIATED? BEYOND "THE MONEY TALK"

> The morality of *rights and abstract reasoning* has been formulated in terms of universal, general principles, whereas the morality of *care and responsibility* has been voiced through narratives that specify fitting responses to proximate situations.[215]

T hese words refer to psychologist Carol Gilligan's distinction between the *justice tradition* for determining what's fair, which reflects the philosophies of male thinkers such as the English Utilitarians and John Rawls, and the *care perspective*, which reflects the more personal, contextual thinking of what she calls woman's "different voice." This distinction colors our discussion in this chapter of whether fairness can be negotiated in family conversations while the parent/testator is still living. What predispositions might participants bring with them? Will some reject the subjective "care and responsibility" approach entirely and insist that only rational, practical and objective rules should prevail? Will others insist that feelings matter? How can this be resolved?

And so the scene shifts once again. We are no longer assembled at the deathbed of a patriarch in the second century BCE ("…in the hour of death, distribute your inheritance") or in the Patrician Assembly of ancient Rome. Nor are we consulting with an attorney in a modern law office. Rather, we are gathered in a family living room or around a table in a small conference room to talk about making or updating our will and other issues. Chief among us is the testator/ estate planner, alone or with spouse or partner, together with adult children and/or partner's children and others who will be affected by our ultimate decisions. Perhaps a facilitator or mediator is on hand as well. The purpose? To inform, yes, but also to listen, acknowledge, learn, and discuss. For this is an exercise in *participatory estate planning,* an attempt to make sure that the *process* is fair from everyone's point of view even if the outcome is not.

"When was the last time you started a conversation about money with your partner, spouse, sibling, children, or parent?" asks financial planner Lori Sackler in her book *The M Word.* "Do you regularly have discussions about money with your family, or do you avoid the topic whenever you can?"[216]

Death, sex, money, politics, religion and Uncle Joe's drinking: all of these topics may be taboo. It's not surprising, then, that for many family members—especially adult children—raising inheritance-related issues with a parent can be uncomfortable, inappropriate, and avoided for a variety of reasons.[217]

Some of us were raised to believe that talking about money was simply impolite. Mixing money with mortality is worse. "Bringing up death would be disrespectful in my family," explains one woman. Some refuse to engage even when a parent wants to talk ("Oh Mom, you're not going to die tomorrow!"). When the query involves not only money but also old age (our dotage?), family relationships, and what's in a parent's will—even whether there *is* a will and where it is stashed—the best-laid plans to talk can be derailed.

Whose responsibility is it to initiate the Money Talk, or, more broadly, the Estate Planning Conversation? A survey by UBS of the Bank's American investors contains a wealth of information about what adult children (potential heirs) know and don't know about their parents' (benefactors') wills and how they feel about it.[218] "Both sides agree that the responsibility lies with the parents to start the conversation," they report. Potential heirs say *they want parents to start inheritance planning early and to include the family in the conversation.* "It's the parents' money and their decision about what to do with it, so it is also up to them to decide when and what to share."

Eighty-three percent of investors sampled had an up-to-date will. Only half of the older parents had discussed their estate plans with their adult children, however. Barriers to discussion arose from both points of view. One-fifth of the older benefactors and half of potential heirs checked the response, "Do not talk about financial issues in our family." One in four on both sides checked "Do not want my children to feel entitled to wealth/Do not want to appear greedy." And although almost all of the benefactors said they want to ensure a "smooth transfer of assets" to their heirs, only two-thirds said they were concerned that "There are no bad feelings among heirs over who got what or how much."

Does knowing ahead of time what is in a parent's will help to alleviate conflict or hurt feelings when the time comes? According to UBS, yes.

When heirs know the details of the inheritance ahead of time—i.e., they've seen the will, know approximately how much wealth there is, how it will be divided and where the assets are—they are much more satisfied with the distribution process.[219]

It is clear that potentially divisive concerns about inheritance need to be resolved *while the testator is alive,* where possible. Of course it is the parent's right not to share information about their estate with their children. But the question remains: is withholding such information fair? Or is there a better way of making decisions—not only *just* but also *caring*—that engages key family members (and perhaps others) in the process and gives everyone an opportunity both to listen and to have their say?

Legal experts differ on how closed or open the process of estate planning should be. At one end of the continuum, Elder Law attorney Mark Accettura urges us to keep the details of our plan *private* except on a need-to-know basis, such as who has financial or health care power of attorney.[220] This is surprising advice in an age in which open communication within families is usually celebrated. But Accettura is clear: estate planning is "autobiographical and undemocratic," he insists. No approval or consensus is needed. And in any case, we might change our minds.

Other advisors urge us to be more open, at least to the extent of *informing* adult children and perhaps other relatives of our financial situation and what we're planning to do. "Families should keep all members in the loop" writes columnist Jane Bryant Quinn.[221] It's fair. It helps to avoid shock and resentment at the end. And there are practical advantages in disclosing in advance what children can expect to receive from our estate. As Sackler reminds us, "They have their own financial planning to do."[222]

Taking it one step further, some experts suggest that not only informing but also inviting and *listening* to adult children's concerns about our intentions is better. "It can even result in useful changes to your plan," says one wealth manager. "I've had personal experience with improving a financial decision because my kids were in the loop."[223]

A more radical option is to put everything on the table in a genuinely *participatory* approach. Conversations could be initiated by the parent(s), by adult children if they have questions or concerns, or by a family lawyer, financial advisor or other professional if they see trouble brewing—or even if they don't. The idea is to engage in a reality check with family members that may help to avoid passing on a legacy of bitterness or hurt feelings, as well as the prospect of litigation before or after our own (or our spouse's or partner's) death. For it's not only the remains of our assets and personal belongings that are at issue here. It's also who we select as administrators, how we expect to spend the remains of our days and, in the end, what happens to our physical remains when we die.

Estate attorneys try to ensure that all relevant options are explored with their clients in the planning process and, ultimately, that everything is in order from the legal point of view: trusts set up, wills signed and witnessed, assets documented, executors and/or trustees appointed, advanced health care directives filled out, powers of attorney assigned, estate and/or inheritance and capital gains taxes considered, personal property memos duly noted, and so on. Originals and copies are made, dated, filed away, and the work is done...for now.

But, behind this orderly facade lurks a potential for disagreement between partners as well as between parents and progeny about what these "relevant options" are. Ideally, spouses will sort out the stickiest issues between them before involving the rest of the family. In an attempt to head off (or at least identify) major sources of contention, attorney Richard Barnes includes a Sample Estate Planning Questionnaire in his book *Estate Planning for Blended Families*.[224] Couples are invited to clarify both their personal financial circumstances and their estate planning hopes and intentions. Although addressed to remarried adults with kids, the process pertains to couples in first marriages as well.

Barnes suggests that each partner individually write down his or her *estate planning goals* ("Your, Yes, YOUR Goals!") and compare priorities. The checklist includes such items as "Providing for your spouse at your death," "Providing for children from your current relationship," "Providing for children from a previous relationship," "Protecting children from losing their inheritance if the surviving spouse remarries," "Keeping a business in the family," "Minimizing estate tax," "Being fair to your spouse, children, and stepchildren in the division of your estate," and "Providing for charity." This exercise is followed by a second checklist of outcomes each partner wants to *avoid*, such as assets coming under the control of a new spouse if the surviving spouse remarries, or children losing their future inheritance to creditors or in their own divorce.

It's possible, of course, that the partners' goals will harmonize perfectly with one another. "However," declares one mediator, "it is dangerous to assume that a 'happily married' couple is communicating well about the division of their estate."[225] Indeed, one can imagine the discord that could reverberate through this drill. "I thought you would leave everything to *me*!" one might say. "How could you do that to your own daughter?" "Don't you trust me?" "Why *him*?"

The nature and balance of the partners' decision-making power and what each knows or believes about his/her/their finances are crucial here. Misperceptions can flourish. Wives, for example—particularly those of older generations or who might have limited experience in the labor force—may be unaware of the specifics of their financial situations ("Oh, my husband has always looked after that"). They may also be less assertive and more vulnerable to being overruled by their husbands, or their husbands' lawyers in a joint visit, than are younger, feistier women or second wives.

What would wives *really* like to do if they had their own way? Gilligan's observation that women tend to make moral choices differently than men do could well extend to their selection of beneficiaries and charitable giving. A woman might favor a special daughter-in-law over an irritating son, for example, or the Humane Society or a grandchild's school over the Elks or VFW. Moreover, as Kate Levinson recounts in her book *Emotional Currency*, women have a different relationship to money than men do. This could well color their decisions about what they would like to give, when, and to whom.

When it comes to communication, too, women and men talk to one another in ways that can bewilder or annoy the other rather than making points clear. In her book *You Just Don't Understand: Women and Men in Conversation*, linguist Deborah Tannen depicts a variety of gendered communication patterns that make us sound like ships passing in the night. Among many examples are a male tendency toward linear decision-making as compared with a female propensity for trying to "make things right" with everyone.[226]

Layered into the couple's planning process and negotiations about fairness are the uncertainties of each spouse's future needs, life expectancies (who is likely to survive the other?) and the mixed prospects of children (his, hers, theirs) and other potential heirs. Given these complexities, it would be prudent for couples to test-run their estate plans with one another and with (perhaps separate) legal counsel before engaging in the Family Conversation—or, more formally, the Mediated Meetings—that are portrayed here. And with the passage of time and change of circumstances, modifications may well be needed.

The goals of an individual estate plan are one thing; the goals of family conversations about them quite another. But the former feeds into the latter. A major function of the participatory process is to provide an opportunity for the testator/estate planner to explain to family members what she or he has been thinking or doing so far, and for participants to know and respond. Explaining the goals of the plan is a start. "I'm preparing my will and making other decisions that affect you," one might say by way of invitation, "and I want to make sure to include you in the conversation."

We don't all need to go whole hog on the transparency idea though. The graduated degrees of privacy or openness about wills and finances in general mentioned earlier can be applied to specific aspects of the estate plan. One could decide in advance what information to keep private, for example; what to share so that everyone is in the know; what is intended to solicit helpful feedback, and what is up for discussion and a possible group decision to get everyone actively on board.

Consider the options. We might simply *announce* what our wishes are about end-of-life medical care, for example, and about the final disposal of our physical remains (organ donation, burial, cremation, funeral or memorial service, religious or not, and so on). The important thing is to ensure that everyone hears from us directly. We don't want any nasty arguments over our dead or dying body.

How to allocate the remains of our real and personal property could be more open, depending on the circumstances. How much information do we want to share about the monetary value of what we have and about what each person is likely to get, how, and when? It's fair to *explain* the basis for our decisions; even better to *invite responses* that may change our minds. Should we be giving gifts now rather than later, if we can afford to, or hold onto everything until we die? Should we set up trusts for our beneficiaries—children, grandchildren, others in the younger generation—to be held until some future date, perhaps with conditions imposed? What does everyone think?

Intentions to bequeath everything to a surviving spouse or to give unequal amounts to natural children or grandchildren are likely to be especially sensitive. So, too, are the needs and expectations of second families or a live-in partner. The appointment of an executor or trustee can also be controversial depending on who it is (an insider, a neutral fiduciary or both?) and the nature of their relationship to heirs, especially if she or he will also benefit. Can family members agree?

What to do with a family residence or vacation home, valuable art works or antiques, a family farm or business, shares in commercial real estate, and other "lumpy" or consequential assets can also generate some heat. According to one expert, the greatest challenges in dividing family property arise from the presence of any or all of four attributes: when it can't be divided easily into shares; when its market value is uncertain; when it is unique; and/or when it holds significant sentimental or symbolic value to at least one family member.[227]

Who wants to keep it; who wants it sold and the proceeds divided? Who is willing to manage and maintain it; who doesn't care? Writing about the transfer of family farms, Janet Taylor and Joan Norris note that, "There is [often] an occupational implication for the next generation: beneficiaries may need to maintain the estate intact in order to maintain profitability; and emotional ties to the land may be very strong."[228] On the other hand, as Sackler reminds us, "Often there is no child who is interested in the family business."[229] This may be true of other real and personal property as well, as much as we value it ourselves. We need to hear this from our potential heirs before we make what could be a costly mistake.

Our offspring may be disappointed by some of what they hear from us, as well. "We're sorry that we can't do more for you, but this is all we have" is one scenario. And here's another: "I've been careful all my life to make sure that I wouldn't become a financial burden to you, and I won't. But now I'd like to do what I've always dreamed of—to leave my money to the organizations I want to support. I hope you'll understand."

Grown children may feel entitled to receive most of what their parents have, whether or not they really need it. Yet, making an estate plan offers an unprecedented opportunity to share what we have with others—to do what we *can* do rather than what others believe we *ought* to do. Our beneficiary could be an institution with special meaning in our lives—a church or university, say—or an organization whose work we especially admire. Or perhaps we would like to remember more distant kin or non-family members in our wills in recognition of past kindness, services rendered, a loving friendship or financial need.

Finally, we will need to discuss what we hope/expect to happen to us in the remains of our days and what plans we have made. Who has—or will be given—our power of attorney for health care decisions and for financial and other matters if/when we are no longer able to act on our own? The duties can be onerous, the decisions hard.

"In my experience," says trust and estate mediator Nancy Powers, "the biggest fights are not about assets as such, but about who will be in charge during the parents' lives when they are no longer serving as their own fiduciaries, or upon a death."[230] Parents and beneficiaries typically have no understanding of the legal responsibilities and time commitments involved, she says, and siblings don't want their sister or brother to be compensated. Family meetings can be used to inform family members about what may be required of them during a parent's declining years or upon death. "Usually," Powers adds, "this information will cause none of the kids to want to be the fiduciary!"

Caring, compensation, control: what assumptions underlie who will do what? Are daughters and daughters-in-law expected to step in with more visits and offers of personal help than are sons? How will family and non-family caregivers and financial overseers be compensated for their time, skills and expenses? Can these questions of fairness be raised in family conversations without threatening the success of the whole endeavor?

When facing the prospect of a Tough Conversation, why not call in the experts?[231] Trained family, elder law and estate planning mediators—some of whom are lawyers—do more than facilitate communication. They help to identify, resolve and prevent family differences with informed and dispassionate support.

A skilled mediator creates an atmosphere of safety and respect, listens deeply to each participant's interests and concerns, and encourages them to hear *and understand* each another. [A mediator] identifies points of agreement and helps the parties to discover one or more mutually acceptable solutions.[232]

A mediator does not (and should not) offer legal advice, however, or arbitrate differences or impose solutions. Like a good doctor, the mediator's function is both preventive and curative. On the preventive side, the mediator solicits participants' viewpoints, identifies sources of disagreement as they arise, and skillfully averts escalation. On the curative side, a mediator helps to reduce harm, reconcile disputes in a non-directive way, and circumvent the financial and emotional costs and unpredictable outcomes of family fights in court. Notes one mediator on this last point:

> Courts are not charged with working out reasonable solutions to heirship contests or disputes over administration of wills and trusts. Judges listen to scripted testimony and make decisions. The results may be cumbersome, with little relief to any party. If the goal is a solution rather than a finding of fault, mediation is the best means to achieve the goal.[233]

Does mediation cost? Yes. Is it likely to be worth it? Yes. As Nancy Powers points out, "The ultra-wealthy are already doing this. They obtain coaching, and use mediation for disputes that may arise along the way. This is necessary and works well because they have complex business interests to protect from protracted litigation that destroys families and dissipates family wealth."[234] But, she adds, middle class families can also afford the costs of mediation involving just a few family meetings. It helps to soften possible conflict, provide valuable information and encourage everyone's cooperation.

Experts offer a wealth of advice on how to have an effective conversation, mediated or not. For author Lori Sackler, the key to a successful Money Talk (or series of talks) is advance planning. Identify the issues, she urges, set the agenda, and select a skilled facilitator. Be sure to ask wrap-up questions at the end to make sure everyone has had their say.

For Robert Mnookin of Harvard Law School's Program on Negotiation, the key is to make sure participants understand what the process is and what their individual and group responsibilities are. Have everyone state their interests and goals directly to one another: equal time, equal say. Participants will insist that they want to be fair, he says. But, as we know, "Terms like *rational* and *fair* can mean radically different things to different people, which itself can be a source of conflict."[235]

Some mediators prefer to hold both individual and joint meetings with participants in order to move the process forward.[236] But others disagree. Mnookin, for example, contends that people see better and listen better in face-to-face sessions. Participants should speak candidly to one another and not rely on indirect messages. In any case, he says, engaging in "shuttle diplomacy" gives the mediator too much power.[237]

Roger Fisher and William Ury, authors of the best-selling book *Getting to Yes*, tell us to start with the issue to be dealt with.[238] Don't bargain over positions; it's inefficient, endangers ongoing relationships and gets people stuck in opposing corners. Rather, discuss one another's perceptions of what's at stake and make sure everyone participates in the process, "listens actively" (everyone says this), and acknowledges (validates) what others have to say.

"What if the 'other side' [think spouse, parent, sibling or other family member] believes in a different standard of fairness?" Fisher and Ury ask. "Explore how these conflicting standards developed," they suggest. "Agreement on the 'best' standard of fairness (equal treatment, reciprocity, tradition, etc.) is *not necessary*."[239] Try to use objective criteria for making decisions such as the market value of various assets, efficiency in settling the estate, or what a court would decide, they say, and discuss how best to maintain a good working relationship.

But, wait! What about these "objective criteria"? Do they trump the more subjective concerns of Gilligan's care perspective? How are these diverse perspectives expressed? Drawing on linguist Deborah Tannen's research, mediators Jan Schau and Nina Meierding demonstrate how different communication styles can impede mutual understanding between the sexes in exactly the type of meetings we are describing here. "Misunderstandings can often occur because of *how* the message is delivered rather than the content or subject matter of the conversation," they observe.[240] In their view, a skilled professional will probe into the client's purpose and/or goal of sharing information and be able to sort this out.

All agree that communication coaches, facilitators or mediators must guarantee a safe and confidential place for participants to share their personal concerns and ideas. They need to make the rules of engagement clear: no challenging, no ridicule, no interruptions, no hostile takeovers, no airing of old grievances. They need to make sure that *the issue* is the issue, not the person, and not control.

Nancy Powers talks with each participant ahead of time to be sure they understand the process and how to be prepared with their questions and concerns. At the meeting(s) she gives everyone a pen and paper so they can jot down what they want to say and not interrupt, assuring all participants that they will get their turn as well as all the time they need to express their thoughts. She calls this "modeling behavior." Powers encourages inclusiveness in such meetings as well.

"No need to create discord and divorces just because the [children's] spouses aren't blood relatives," she says. Others agree. "The inclusion of some and not others could cause bad feelings, retaliation, or unwanted confrontations," explains one California judge.[241]

It is important to note that mediated family estate planning does not necessarily end with a legally binding agreement. The participants might generate some sort of informal go-ahead or memo of understanding as a *guide*, but not as a solution. Facilitation and mediation are not arbitration, and no one is legally bound by the outcome unless they all agree. Ideally, the process will lead to some consensus about—or at least a better understanding of—the issues at hand among all concerned. Ideally, too, most participants will concede that the procedure is fair. But when it comes to the final settlement, the decisions do not belong to family members, neither the most persuasive among them nor all of them in collusion. Nor do they belong to the estate attorney, financial advisor, mediator, facilitator, or coach. For in the end—as in the beginning in ancient Rome—the decision belongs to the maker of the will and owner of the estate.

In his book *Blood and Money: Why Families Fight About Inheritance,* attorney Mark Accettura tells of "toxic testators" who act out of punitive motives. But it's not only abuse that can be toxic; it's also carelessness and neglect. The attitude of "Let them sort it out after I'm gone: it's not my problem" leaves heirs anxious, bereft, and even furious. "Why didn't Dad even *ask* us if that's what we wanted? Didn't he *care?*" is one case in point. "Where is everything we *need?* It will take months to go through all this stuff to find what we're looking for!" is another. Amidst all of the contradictions of what is fair or just that are reviewed in this book, here is at least one point of clarity: passing on to our survivors the information they need to settle our (and their) affairs is fair; leaving them in the dark or with a mess to deal with after we're gone is not.

"Obviously, you want to keep all these documents in a safe place, where you, and your executor or successor trustee, can readily find them" writes attorney Denis Clifford in *Plan Your Estate.*[242] (This advice follows more than four hundred pages of details about wills, codicils, trusts, tax laws, executors and trustees, powers of attorney and other legal matters.) But if we are to be genuinely *fair* as well as kind and considerate to our executors, successor trustees, and family and close friends who survive us, we need to gather more together—indeed, much more—where they can easily find it. Some of this information is purely practical (where are the keys, the passwords, the insurance papers, the pink slip for the car?). Some is emotional, encompassing our personal histories and family lore. Like an anthropological dig, let's think of this collection of information as constituting three tiers of our contemporary equivalent of bones and pottery shards.

In the first tier are the signed, witnessed and dated legal documents with instructions about our medical and final wishes, durable powers of attorney, and the settling of our estate, however modest it may be. Presumably we have already shared these instructions with our executors and family members so they know what to do, both before and after we die.

The second tier contains multiple pieces of practical information about who we are and where to find everything that is needed to report our death to the authorities and to settle our affairs. Among many helpful manuals for gathering this material is Sally Balch Hurme's *Checklist for My Family: A Guide to My History, Financial Plans, and Final Wishes* published by AARP and the American Bar Association.[243]

Hurme's book includes useful worksheets for transcribing our personal and family biographical data and documents (birth, adoption, marriage and divorce certificates, passport, drivers' license and social security numbers, etc.); guardianship of minor children or other dependents as well as pets; professional advisors (tax accountant, attorney, financial consultant, insurance agent, etc.); service providers, caregivers, domestic workers, employers or employees, etc.; plus personal contacts (friends, relatives, members of clubs or organizations we belong to, work colleagues) and others who need to be notified.

Add to this the locations of essential items (keys, storage units, safety deposit boxes, security codes, credit cards, computers, passwords, etc.); insurance policies, retirement and veterans benefits statements; state and federal tax filings; checking and savings accounts; investment reports, real estate titles and assessments; other assets and/or income and debts such as mortgages, credit card balances, and statements due; vehicles (registration of cars, trucks, motorcycles); medical records; and so on. This may seem like a lot. But most American households have acquired at least some of these assets (and debts), if not all. And many will also have "digital assets" to which fiduciaries need to have access if they are to be passed on or destroyed according to the owner's wishes.

The third tier of this archeological depository contains a rich layer of personal wishes, instructions, commentary, and family lore for our survivors that give special meaning to our lives and to theirs. Psychologist Tina Cole Kreitz calls this *The Last Gift Box: A Present to Those Who Follow Me.*[244] This is where imagination and creativity kick in. Kreitz's workbook asks for all sorts of details relating to our death, funeral and memorial wishes; how we would like to be remembered; whether we'd like our survivors to hold a party for us with music, food and drink; where this might be, who to invite, and so on. And there are gifts of the surprising kind. "One of the nicest gifts you can give your children and family is to select and prepay for your cemetery plot, mausoleum or cremation." (There are less expensive and less binding arrangements than "package deals" by the funeral industry, however.) Put together everything they'll need to write an obituary, if they'll need one, or write it yourself. Include some humor, stories, things you would like people to remember you for. A photo, of how you (once) looked.

Of great importance are the family treasures, heirlooms and keepsakes, no matter how modest. Be sure to attach stories of their meaning, value and provenance; objects without stories can lose their soul and look like nothing special. "YOU decide what items go to each child, family member, friend," says Kreitz. At the same time, "It is important to give our children and our siblings permission to sell items if they are not wanted by anyone or if the family needs the money for their well-being."[245]

We may have saved old letters, personal journals, genealogies, photographs, report cards and diplomas, children's art, baby books, newspaper clippings, things we have written. Perhaps they will not mean much to a second spouse or to younger generations. But we should resist the temptation to toss everything out as we downsize, experts advise. Ask before selling, giving away or disposing of things. And don't make assumptions about who might or might not want to keep what or, for that matter, about anything else regarding our own passing or what we pass on to others.

Finally, think about writing an "ethical will." Deriving from ancient oral Judeo-Christian tradition, ethical wills are intended to pass on to descendants the blessings, lessons, instructions, observations, philosophies and spiritual values of the deceased. We don't need to go that far ourselves. But the idea of revealing our thoughts to a selected few, preferably in hand-written letters, has its appeal—at least for some.

"Don't get caught up in the perfect paper or card or word," urges Kreitz. "This is a letter, not an epic, not a test." The ancient art of transmitting ethical instructions to future generations has morphed into a less formal mode of communication. But one could still use this as an opportunity to set down in writing the ideas and concerns and wishes that inform our legacy.[246] It's not meant to be a stern moral lecture, as in times past, or a contemporary greeting card from the Beyond. Rather, it can be an account of what we tried to achieve in our lives and an expression of our hopes for those we leave behind.

And so it is that we plan for our demise. We have been presented with many points of view in this book regarding what's fair in family inheritance and what's not. Some appear difficult to reconcile: contradictions between individual freedom and social responsibility, for example; between private accumulation and the public good; between the morality of rights and abstract reasoning and the morality of care and responsibility. But balances can be struck; that is part of the challenge.

We have been presented, too, with choosing between equity and equality in bequests within families when the two are not congruent; with managing both procedural and distributive justice in the way we handle our estates; with deciding what to discuss with our heirs before we die and what to keep to ourselves, and more. What are we to make of all of these options?

In response, let's think of the planning process as a series of conversations. This book includes the views of a number of "great thinkers"—of historians, economists and philosophers debating the larger questions of social justice—and of academic researchers, journalists, estate planners and other professionals engaged in the more practical aspects of inheritance law and practice. Perhaps we have been having conversations with each of them as we were reading, nodding our heads or mentally arguing back. Perhaps we have also been having conversations with our families, friends, lawyers, pastors, and others to whom we turn for information and advice. By now there are undoubtedly many voices in the room, sometimes all talking at once.

There is a purpose to this exercise, however. It is not just to expose us to multiple points of view, as interesting as that can be. It's also to offer some conceptual tools for *identifying what we ourselves believe and would like to do.* Creating a comprehensive estate plan involves making numerous moral choices that we may not be prepared for, especially if we're in a state of denial about our own death or that of a beloved partner. The ideas presented here are intended to help us to explore, rethink and clarify the reasoning behind the choices that we make. Why are we choosing this and not that? What are our values and our goals, and how are they shaping what we decide to do?

Wills are not simply legal formalities that we should carry out and then hide away to "lie dormant for years, and then spring to life when their author dies, as if death were rain."[247] Rather, they are living documents whose potentially explosive contents need to be carefully thought through, revised and updated. Throughout this sequence of events we may change our minds, our values, our wishes, or we may not. Ultimately, it is up to each of us to listen to our inner voices—to have *conversations with ourselves*—as the final guide to preparing our Last Will and Testament. That is what the privilege and the duty of testamentary freedom allow us to do.

And at the end of his days, Jacob said to his sons,[248]

I am to be gathered unto my people: bury me with my fathers in the cave that is in the field of Ephron the Hittite.... And when Jacob had made an end of commanding his sons, he gathered up his feet into the bed, and yielded up the ghost, and was gathered unto his people.

Practical Attorney-Client Strategies for Creating a Fair Estate Plan

E mpowered with the knowledge that you have full autonomy in designing your own estate plan, and inspired by this book's exhortations that the fundamental values of fairness should be integrated into your decision making, you are now embarked on the journey towards translating these core principles into reality. As so many of my clients have told me—or, more painfully, as many others have demonstrated in the conflicts they leave behind when they haven't addressed these concerns properly—it's not a simple job. It requires a high degree of emotional courage, a careful curating of the appropriate professional team, and a keen ability to translate your unique and often complex personal family constellations into practical and enforceable testamentary documents.

Comprehending the full dimension of these tasks is something that every professional working in this field also needs to master. The suggestions set forth here are meant to inspire the lawyers and financial planners working in this field as well as their clients. Oftentimes we have witnessed, with sometimes disastrous results, how a narrowly focused attorney, who thinks only of minimizing tax payments or keeping the estate plan simple, can end up discouraging the client—who is the true decision-maker—from making emotionally intelligent decisions. Drafting a will or trust is truly a team effort. It will be a winning game only if both sides of the attorney-client team are on board with a congruent set of values and goals.

P lanning ahead—first steps: The first component of the estate pre-planning process—and one that is ignored by far too many testators—involves who in a relationship is going to participate in making the decisions. Whether or not the assets are owned separately or jointly, a married couple (or any couple in a long-term partnership) needs to ensure that both of them are engaged in the process. At the same time, each partner or spouse will likely have separate areas of concern. Some of their assets may be separately owned (or part of a family inheritance from one partner's family), and they may well have different dependents, different priorities and different goals.

This situational difference is especially true for blended families, where each spouse might have children from a prior relationship. But it also can occur when one partner has a former spouse or partner, or a parent or sibling who requires special consideration. Conferring with one's spouse or partner is essential in the decision-making process. But be warned: this is likely to be complicated, as it can open fissures in the relationship. Nor is it always easy to balance coordination with one's partner and autonomous decision-making.

The second component of the pre-planning process involves the challenging question of how to best engage (or not) the potential recipients of one's bounty. There is a wide range of options here. Some folks prefer to keep their estate plans entirely to themselves, even until death, in the belief that their heirs will likely understand the reasoning behind them (or at a minimum, they will have no choice but to accept them). At the other extreme, others elect to open the discussion from the outset with everyone who will be affected. In between lies a range of possibilities, from lengthy discussions with some heirs and not others, for example, and from vague comments to full details with requests for feedback. Recognizing that there is no single right answer, it's best to start with a few incremental discussions, one at a time, asking your children (or other likely heirs) whether they want to participate in a full family conversation about the issues. Along the way it's prudent to confer with your attorney or professional team about how you are managing the process. But remember, *you* are in charge, not them.

In most instances the structure of the decision-making conversations will flow from the particulars of your situation. If your main asset is a family business and you are evaluating who should control it upon your death, it is essential that you include those who will be responsible for its management. In contrast, if it's a matter of who is going to receive your investment assets, detailed conversations with your heirs are not so crucial. So too, if all of the intended heirs are fairly similarly situated financially, then there's less need for a family discussion. But if one or more of your children is in particularly bad straits, if some children have been more involved with your care than others, or if you anticipate dissension among your family members regarding the plan, talking it through is of critical importance.

The ingredients of such a conversation are well covered in Chapter Six of this book. From my perspective as an attorney there are two frequently recurring scenarios that pose the greatest challenges. The first arises when there's a late-in-life new romance, where the new partner (married or otherwise) is financially dependent and the testator's legitimate desire to take care of that partner conflicts with the expectations of his (or her) children from a prior marriage. Depending on the size of the estate this can truly be a "zero sum game" in which the funds needed by the surviving partner suck up nearly all of the estate's assets. Doubts and anxieties are bound to surface regarding the parent's loyalty to his or her children; the role of the new partner in the care of (and possible control over) the aging parent; the children's suspicion and resentment of the new partner as a gold-digger or interloper in the family; and, possibly, remarks from the parent that hint at disregard (or even dislike) of the former spouse. There's no simple way of navigating these waters. In extreme cases, calling in a family counselor or mediator can be very useful.

Another scenario arises where there are serious doubts as to the emotional or financial competence of a likely heir, such that some serious restrictions on the inherited assets make good legal sense. It can be very difficult to decide how to distribute the assets and to set up a trustee arrangement that is realistic and effective. Except for the relatively simple situation where there is a physical disability, in most instances the likely heir will not be happy to hear about any restrictions and may well be enraged by their imposition in the estate plan. Inherent in their emotional response will be a rejection of the core judgment behind the plan, such that in some instances it may be best to leave them out of the discussion entirely.

The third component of the pre-planning process involves selecting your professional team if you don't have one already, such as an attorney, financial advisor, and accountant. It is not just a matter of finding a lawyer with legal competence: that's essential for every legal task, and we assume you will limit your choices to well-respected estate planners. What is less obvious is how to select a counselor who is willing and able to engage with you on the higher-level task of developing a fair and emotionally intelligent estate plan, that is, one that recognizes and takes into account your own and your potential heirs' emotions and builds on that information appropriately and constructively. To my surprise I have discovered that many estate attorneys have little interest in this dimension of the legal task; some are even hostile to the subject. To some, emotions are like the Grand Canyon: they fear that if they stray too close to the edge they will fall off! Given this dynamic, you want to be clear from the outset that you intend to take the issues of fairness seriously. Moreover, you want to work with someone who is not only open to these discussions, but also has a level of emotional intelligence as a professional that adds value to the conversation. Be sure to bring up these issues in the first intake session with your lawyer or when you return for an update. If you hit a wall of resistance or disinterest, choose a different attorney.

The final piece of the puzzle involves the selection of your trustee or executor. This is never a simple decision, and no one should assume that the beneficiaries or the spouse or children are the best suited for this task. In part it depends on the nature of your estate and your testamentary plan. If there are trusts for younger children that will be administered over time, or business assets that need to be managed, this will require a higher level of competence for a trustee. If the beneficiaries are prone to conflict and distrust, finding a friend, relative or professional advisor who can manage the distribution process will be essential. Don't surprise your trustee at the last minute: make sure you confer with them in advance of the selection, to be sure they are on board with your plans.

D eciding on your beneficiaries: Once your team is in place and you have decided how to approach the family discussions, your first step in designing a fair estate plan—with an eye to minimizing the future problems of an unfair plan—is to engage in an open and honest discussion with your advisors about the reality of each of your children's individual situations, as well as the needs of your larger community of dependents or likely heirs. As part of that initial conversation, you should also explore the broadest range of your social concerns so that you can evaluate the role of charitable bequests in your estate plan.

For those who have children, in most instances there will be an intersecting overlay of emotional and financial dynamics for each particular child that needs to be faced without distortion or avoidance. The questions each family needs to ask will differ, based upon the particular financial and living conditions for each child, but generally involve such issues as who has been successful or unsuccessful in their lives and why; who has special needs; who has been especially helpful to the parents during their times of need; and what gifts each child has already received or is likely to receive in the future (e.g., inheritances from another source).

Clearly this process involves more than just surveying the financial net worth of each child or potential heir. The emotional perspectives and the relative positions of each child in relationship to your aging process are also key parts of the landscape. In this territory, the most frequently recurring dynamic is that of the "dutiful" child who may have developed a sense of entitlement arising out of his or her actual (or perceived) dedication to your care. It is no coincidence that oftentimes the most financially needy child is the one who is available to help, as she or he is likely to be the one without a demanding career or a large extended family that commands attention. Thus, the more attentive daughter may feel strongly that she should inherit your house as compensation for all the years of care she provided whereas her siblings might feel, with some justification, that the free rent and financial assistance given to her all these many years results, if anything, in a debt to the estate.

Remember, it is not your job to issue any final "rulings" on these disparate points of view, but rather, to acknowledge all of these points of view in approaching your final decisions. What is most essential is that you and your advisors face these conditions and expectations openly, engaging in a discussion that encompasses all of the uncertainties and contradictions and unpredictable trajectories as part of your decision-making process.

Most estate planners assume that the "right" plan bequeaths everything to a spouse if you are married, and then gives each child an equal share of the estate upon the death of your spouse. Rather than start with this sort of presumed structure, I think it makes better sense to consider each potential heir individually, balancing out that person's needs and interests—and *earned* entitlements—as a separate concern.

Focusing on each individual's situation first will force you to think more deeply about that person's real-life predicaments and opportunities, and will bring to mind your own feelings and opinions about their situation. And along the way, embark on the same exploration with regard to potential charities or personal causes, as well as potential beneficiaries who are not part of your immediate family. As noted earlier in this book, these can include siblings, nieces and nephews, and other relatives; children of a partner or spouse; former partners or spouses; close friends who have become like family to you; colleagues, neighbors or long-term employees; favorite charities or "causes" of personal importance; and community institutions that further your personal values. At this initial stage of the review it isn't necessary to assign particular assets or percentages to each person or cause. Instead, you are focused solely on your attitudes about each potential beneficiary—whether individual or entity—so that you can integrate those feelings into the comprehensive plan you are going to make.

Then, having surveyed the broadest of fields of prospective beneficiaries, you can decide who (or what entity) to eliminate from the plan altogether, and who or what to prioritize. Narrowing your list will greatly simplify your task, as then you can move on to considering the particular needs of each recipient and on the limits you want to impose on each bequest. That is the time for deciding how to address the dilemma of having one child who is financially responsible while the other is wildly reckless: do you make an outright gift to the responsible kid but hold back the other child's inheritance in a trust managed by a professional or a family member? Another recurring problem is how to address excess gifts made during your lifetime: do you adjust the inheritance plan to equalize or balance out those gifts to any degree, or do you consider those prior gifts as having been made in consideration of pressing needs at the time of the gift, and make equal bequests notwithstanding the prior gifts?

P assing on your assets: There are three basic methods of passing assets to your heirs upon your death: titling of an account or a property, signing a will, or creating a trust and transferring your assets into your trust. Each method has particular advantages and limitations, and so you will need to give close consideration as to which is best for you, and which method works for each bequest.

The simplest method of passing an asset to an heir is with a "transferable upon death" or joint tenancy account or title. You can do this by *titling the asset* (e.g. bank account, real estate) as joint tenants with the intended heir, who as co-owner automatically assumes a "right of survivorship." The downside of using this method, and it's a big downside, is that legally speaking your heir is a co-owner of the asset while you are still alive, and you can't change the designation without her or his consent. In some extreme situations your co-owner might even demand a share of the asset while you are alive. Thus, you don't want to use this technique unless you are perfectly comfortable co-owning the asset or account with your intended heir now.

A better titling method is the "transfer upon death" designation. This keeps the asset solely in your name while you are alive, and allows you to change the designation without the consent (or even the knowledge) of the designated heir and even to sell or spend the entirety of the asset during your lifetime if you wish. In some states you can use this method only to pass bank accounts on to an heir; in other states you can also use it for real estate assets. If most or all of your assets allow for such a designation, it is the simplest and least expensive method of passing an asset to a particular person (or group of heirs) upon your death.

The second transfer method is via a *will*, which is simply a written document that instructs your executor to distribute your assets according to its terms upon your death. Wills can be written without the aid of an attorney: many online tools are available to create one. There are two downsides to using a will, however. Unless your estate is very small, your executor will have to process the distribution through the court probate system. This can be time-consuming and expensive in some states. Each state has its own minimum thresholds for imposing court probate. But even where probate isn't a concern, you can't set up any complicated arrangements for bequests using a will. Thus, if you want to create a plan that allows one child to reside in the house but allocates expenses otherwise, or distributes funds to an heir over time under set conditions, you won't be able to use a simple will, but instead will need to prepare a living (revocable) trust. The same rule applies if you want to leave your house and some of your assets to your new partner during his or her lifetime, but also to mandate where those assets go upon your partner's death. If you are using a will, then you will need to appoint an executor to carry out its terms.

The third and most complex arrangement is to create a living (revocable) *trust*. A trust is simply a legal entity that you create. It holds title to your assets while you are alive, typically under your control as long as you are competent. In the event of your disability, incompetence or death, it designates someone else (known as a successor trustee) to distribute the assets to your heirs as you have set forth in the trust document. The main advantages of a trust are the mirror image of the downsides of a will: you don't need to process the distribution through the court system, and you can set up far more complex mechanisms of distribution. You can instruct your trustee to distribute the assets slowly over time, and you can allow one heir (such as a spouse) to use an asset during his or her lifetime, and direct who gets the asset upon his or her death. The main negative of a trust is that it costs more in legal fees to set up than does a simple will, and you probably shouldn't be doing it yourself or with an on-line form. The additional downside is that you have to transfer your assets into the trust for it to be effective, which means changing the titles of your assets to that of the trust. Depending on the nature of your assets, this can be a rather complicated task.

Keep in mind that most estate plans become stale over time and need to be re-evaluated. Family dynamics change, financial needs change, and the scale of your assets is likely to change over the years. All three methods of estate planning have their own technical requirements for such updates, and each will involve a visit to your lawyer and a bit (or quite a bit) more in legal fees.

Now that you know roughly what is involved in operationalizing a fair estate plan, the process can proceed as follows:

First, survey your particular field of family members, prospective heirs, and worthy causes, and come to some preliminary decisions about how you want to structure your estate plan.

Second, assemble your team, which will include your partner or spouse if you have one, an estate attorney, and possibly a financial advisor and/or an accountant. At some point in the process you will need to add to the team your designated executor or trustee.

Third, meet with your professional team to learn about the best methods of implementing your estate plan, and to identify any particular points of uncertainty or tax or financial consequences for your particular plan. At the same time, present your attorney with your general set of intentions so that you can learn whether there are potential downsides to your approach.

Fourth, discuss your plan with your family members and close advisors, where appropriate, to listen to their concerns and reflect on potential defects or changes you might wish to make.

Fifth, adjust your conceptual plan with the input from your personal advisors and meet again with your estate planner. Explain your plan to your lawyer, and authorize him or her to draft documents consistent with what you want to do.

Sixth, review, revise, finalize, approve and then sign your testamentary documents, and take whatever legal steps are necessary (such as trust transfer deeds) to make it work.

Clients often ask what is their deadline for completing their estate plan. The answer I give is always a simple one: make sure it gets done before you die! Since no one can ever be certain when that fateful event will occur, the takeaway message is, Get started now and proceed with all deliberate speed! And if you already have a will or trust socked away somewhere from long ago, bring it out, look it over, and make sure it still represents your situation and your wishes.

A note to attorneys: In order to be effective in this process, it is vital that you open yourself up to these discussions in all their dimensions. Be prepared to signal your openness—indeed, your eagerness—to engage in this process. It is assumed that you know the procedural rules of your state that control how assets are transferred upon death, as well as the tax issues that will apply to the particular estate you are planning. But in order for your plan to be truly effective, you will need to ask the appropriate questions about your clients' family circumstances and then be willing to talk openly about how best to integrate that reality into their testamentary plan.

Since the goal of any estate plan is to distribute the assets in an efficient *and equitable* manner, knowing the details of your client's family landscape is an essential component of a good legal plan. While it is rarely taught in law school or any advance courses on estate planning, estate planners or financial consultants can be effective only when they have a realistic assessment of these personal conditions and know how to integrate these dynamics into the estate plan. It is entirely appropriate—and in fact, professionally mandated—that the advisor explore these stories with their clients. Gathering this information is not simply a matter of avoiding malpractice (though that should always be a concern); it's an important element of providing professionally competent services.

Articulating this professional responsibility to the client serves as strong justification for requesting such sensitive information. Here is how I suggest you deliver the message: "I'm not here to judge your kids; rather, I'm required to know this information so that I can advise you on how best structure your estate plan." A colleague puts it more simply: "Tell me about your family and what's important to you," she says. "What do I need to know that will help me to help you create a better estate plan?"

Encouraging your clients to talk openly about these stories at your very first meeting can point you in the direction you need to go. You can then integrate the likely ramifications of these family dynamics into your discussions of the appropriate structure of the estate plan, as well as the intended distribution of the assets. Once you know where the emotional and practical landmines are located, you can use your legal skills to design a plan that takes these challenges into account. Don't be afraid to ask, "Do you think that's fair? Why? Can you explain your reasoning?" Or even, "How do you think your heirs might react to this plan? Have you talked with them about it?" The same sets of questions apply to the selection of executors and trustees. You will want to ascertain whether they are sufficiently skillful in both the practical and emotional dynamics of implementing the estate plan, and capable of weathering the potential storms that can arise during the asset distribution process.

There may be some awkward moments in the conversation, but chances are your clients will truly appreciate your guidance. Of greatest importance, it is much more likely that the resulting estate plan will better serve their needs, and the needs of their heirs.

Introduction

1. Pew Research Center, "The Sandwich Generation: Rising Financial Burdens for Middle-Aged Americans," www.pewsocialtrends.org/files/2013/01/Sandwich_Generation_Report_FINAL_1-29.pdf and "Most Middle-Aged Adults Are Rethinking Retirement Plans," www.pewsocialtrends.org/2009/05/28/most-middle-aged-adults-are-rethinking-retirement-plans/.

2. Jeffrey M. Jones, "Majority in U.S. Do Not Have a Will," www.gallup.com/poll/191651/majority-not.aspx.

3. Janet Malcolm, *Two Lives: Gertrude and Alice* (Yale University Press, 2008), 201-202.

Chapter One

4. Jans Beckert, *Inherited Wealth* (Princeton University Press, 2008), 1.

5. Ralph C. Brashier, *Inheritance Law and the Evolving Family* (Philadelphia: Temple University Press, 2004), 91.

6. Denis Clifford, *Plan Your Estate* (Nolo, 2016), 37-50.

7. For stories of battles over the wills of famous people see P. Mark Accettura, *Blood & Money: Why Families Fight over Inheritance and What to Do About It* (Collinwood Press, 2011), 83-124.

8. Melanie B. Leslie, "The Myth of Testamentary Freedom," *Arizona Law Review* 38 (1996). The probate of a will means proving its validity in court. As a general rule, a will has no legal effect until it has gone through this process. In intestacy cases, probate courts appoint administrators to settle the estate according to the relevant statutes, including those relating to descent and distribution.

9. *Duhaime's Law Dictionary,* "Testamentary Freedom," www.duhaime/ org/Legal/Dictionary.

10. Mary Ann Glendon and Max Rheinstein, "Inheritance Law," *Encyclopaedia Brittanica* (2015).

11. "Twelve Tables, Table V," https://www.brittanica.com/topic/Roman-law.

12. This condition was to last for one thousand years until the emperor Justinian published a greatly revised *Corpus Juris Civilis* in 543 to 548 CE that legitimized bilateral descent and the rights of wives and daughters to inherit.

13. Henry Sumner Maine, *Ancient Law, Its Connection with the Early History of Society, and Its Relation to Modern Ideas* (London: Dent, 1965; first published 1861), 131.

14. Maine, *Ancient Law,* 128, emphasis in the original.

15. Maine, *Ancient Law,* 131.

16. Lifetime tenants had earlier been granted ownership and the right to sell their land, with some restrictions.

17. In 1670, Parliament approved a Statute of Distribution for moveable (personal) property in intestacy cases that differs significantly from the rules relating to landed property. Following a different evolutionary path, the Statute codified practices long followed by the ecclesiastical courts that were drawn from the Roman Emperor's reworking of inheritance and family laws in the sixth century. Unless instructed otherwise, a man's moveable property was to be divided equally among his children regardless of birth order and gender if his wife did not survive him. A widow would receive one-third share and the children two-thirds. Absent children, the widow received one-half and the other half passed to the father of the deceased or to a brother or sister. These guidelines became the model for legislation in the

United States. See Mary Ann Glendon and Max Rheinstein, "Intestate Succession," *Encyclopaedia Brittanica* (2015).

18. J. M. W. Bean, *The Decline of English Feudalism, 1215-1540* (Manchester University Press, 1968), 293 (emphasis added). See also Accettura, *Blood & Money*, 244-45, and Beckert, *Inherited Wealth*, 69.

19. Carole Shammas, "Re-Assessing the Married Women's Property Acts," *Journal of Women's History* 6 (1994).

20. See Zouheir Jamoussi, *Primogeniture and Entail in England* (Cambridge Scholars Publishing, 2011), among other sources.

21. Lee J. Alston and Morton Owen Schapiro, "Inheritance Law Across Colonies: Causes and Consequences," *Journal of Economic History* 44 (1984), 278. New England colonies in this classification are Maine, New Hampshire, Vermont, Massachusetts, Plymouth, Rhode Island and Connecticut; Middle Colonies are New York, New Jersey, Pennsylvania and Delaware; South Colonies are Maryland, Virginia, North Carolina, South Carolina and Georgia.

22. Alston and Schapiro, "Inheritance Law Across Colonies," 279.

23. Not 1925 did the British Parliament eliminate primogeniture from the intestacy statutes.

24. Beckert, *Inherited Wealth*, 114-115.

25. Beckert, *Inherited Wealth*, 150.

26. In his will, Washington explains why he cannot return to Martha the "dower slaves" that she brought into the marriage. They are to be freed only at her death along with his own.

27. https://www.tjheritage.org/will-of-thomas-jefferson.

28. https://founders.archives.gov/documents/Washington/06-04-02-0404-0001.

29. Shammas, "Re-assessing the Married Women's Property Acts," 9 (emphasis added); see also Carole Shammas, Marylynn Salmon and Michel

Dahlin, *Inheritance in America: From Colonial Times to the Present* (Rutgers University Press, 1987) and Joan R. Gundersen, "Women and Inheritance in America" in Inheritance and Wealth in America, ed. Robert K. Miller, Jr. and Stephen J. McNamee (New York: Plenum Press, 1998).

30. Shammas, "Re-assessing the Married Women's Property Acts," 11.

31. Archival records from various locales during the colonial period (from 1660 to 1774, well before the Acts) reveal that between 3 and 9 percent of probated estates belonged to female decedents, primarily widows, accounting for 2 to 6 percent of total probated wealth (Shammas, "Re-assessing the Married Women's Property Acts," 16-20). From 1790 to 1922, the proportions of estates with female decedents rose sporadically and unevenly, state by state, reaching 25 percent in one national sample from 1922. By the 1950s, women's estates reached one-third of the total; by now, they would be about half. A 1994 national survey found that women aged 70 and over were only slightly less likely than men that age to have written a will, at 67 and 72 percent, respectively (Angel, *Inheritance in Contemporary America*, 56).

32. Until the passage of the Equal Credit Opportunity Act in 1974, most U.S. banks required single, widowed or divorced women to bring a man along to cosign any credit application, regardless of their income. Married women did not have the legal right to obtain a credit card in their own name.

33. Accettura, *Blood & Money*, 42; Beckert, *Inherited Wealth*, 91.

34. Accettura, *Blood & Money*, 41.

35. Some state intestacy laws are at *www.nolo.com/legal-encyclopedia/intestate-succession*.

36. For Canadian provinces see Wikipedia, "Inheritance Law in Canada; Interstate Succession." Accettura, *Blood & Money*, 247.

37. Accettura, *Blood & Money*, 250.

38. National Conference of Commissioners on Uniform State Laws, *Uniform Probate Code (1969) (Amended 2010)*. www.uniformlaws.org.

39. Marie Louise Fellows, Rita J. Simon and William Rau, "Public attitudes about property distribution at death and intestate property succession laws in the United States," *Law and Social Inquiry* 3 (1978).

40. Marvin B. Sussman, Judith N. Cates and David T. Smith, *The Family and Inheritance* (New York: Russell Sage Foundation, 1970), 147-8.

41. Accettura, *Blood & Money*, 248-9 (emphasis added).

42. Shammas, Salmon and Dahlin, *Inheritance in America*, 207

43. Forced heirship is not recognized in Canada, the United States or Australia or in England, Ireland, Wales, China, Hong Kong Mexico, South Africa, South Korea or Singapore. See Julie Garber, "Forced Heirship," https://www.thebalance.com/forced-heirship-3505530, "Summary of key succession regimes."

44. The Napoleonic Code still holds force in Louisiana, a former French colony.

45. Among countries that practice forced succession to at least a partial extent (that is, as applied to most if not all of the total value of the estate) are France, Germany, Ireland, Italy, Switzerland, and Spain in Europe; the Russian Federation; Turkey, Saudi Arabia and Indonesia (the latter with Civil Code and Islamic Law as applicable); Japan; and Argentina, Brazil, the Dominican Republic, and Venezuela (but not Mexico). See Garber, "Forced Heirship," "Summary of key succession regimes."

46. Garber, "Forced Heirship," 1.

47. Anthony B. Atkinson, *Inequality: What Can Be Done?* (Cambridge MA: Harvard University Press, 2015),160. Atkinson's exact wording is "In France and many other countries, one cannot leave all one's wealth to a donkey sanctuary."

48. Pierre Pestieau, *The Role of Gift and Estate Transfers in the United States and Europe*, www.crepp.ulg.ac.be/papers/crepp-wp200202.pfd, 3.

49. Interestingly, Japan adopted the German Code and Turkey the Swiss Code (Editors of Encylopaedia Britannica, "Napoleonic Code").

50. Glendon and Rheinstein, "Intestate Succession."

51. Beckert, *Inherited Weath*, 70.

52. Marx continues, "In England, the will as such goes back a very long way, nor can there be the slightest doubt that the Anglo-Saxons adopted it from Roman jurisprudence" (Karl Marx and Frederick Engels, *Collected Works, Volume 41* (London: Lawrence and Wishart, 1985), 317. Engels, too, casts testamentary freedom as patriarchal power in his book *The Origin of the Family, Private Property and the State* first published in 1884 (Penguin Classics, 2010), 79 (emphasis added). "In the countries where an obligatory share of the paternal inheritance is secured to the children by law and they cannot therefore be disinherited—in Germany, in the countries with French law and elsewhere—the children are obliged to obtain their parents' consent to their marriage. In the countries with English law, where parental consent to a marriage is not legally required, the parents on their side have full freedom in the testamentary disposal of their property *and can disinherit their children at their pleasure.* It is obvious that, in spite and precisely because of this fact, freedom of marriage among the classes with something to inherit is in reality not a whit greater in England and America than it is in France and Germany" (emphasis added).

53. Beckert, *Inherited Wealth*, 21, 62-3.

54. The Napoleonic Code replaced a collection of regional and local laws, customs and practices adopted from Roman law, feudal Frankish and Germanic institutions, the cannon law of the Roman Catholic Church, royal decrees and acts of parliament. Created as a "purely rational" law, it was to be "free from all past prejudices," deriving its

"moral justification...not in ancient custom or monarchical paternalism but in its conformity to the dictates of reason ..." (Editors, *Encyclopaedia Britannica,* "Napoleonic Code." www.britannica/com/topic/Napoleonic-Code).

Chapter Two

55. John Cunliffe and Guido Erreygers, eds., *Inherited Wealth, Justice and Equality* (London and new York: Routledge, 2013), 1.

56. Manuel Velasquez et al., "Justice and Fairness," Markula Center for Applied Ethics, Santa Clara University, 2014), 2.

57. Velasquez et al., "Justice and Fairness," 3 (emphases added). For a major treatment of the concepts in political philosophy see John Rawls, *Justice as Fairness: A Restatement* (Cambridge, MA: Harvard University Press, 2001).

58. Cited in Atkinson, *Inequality: What Can Be Done?* 13.

59. Compiled from several dictionary definitions.

60. Velasquez et al., "Justice and Fairness," 2, emphases added.

61. Carol Hamilton, "Why did Jefferson change 'property' to the 'pursuit of happiness'?" HistoryNewsNetwork.org/article/46460.

62. Beckert, *Inherited Wealth,* 73; see also Ronald Chester, *Inheritance, Wealth, and Society* (Bloomington IN: Indiana University Press, 1982), 13-21.

63. At www.constitution.org/bor/amd_jmad.htm.

64. Robert K. Miller, Jr. and Stephen J. McNamee, eds., *Inheritance and Wealth in America* (New York: Plenum Press), 1-2.

65. Amartya Sen, *The Idea of Justice* (Cambridge, MA: Belknap Press, 2009), 10. This is a particular critique of two principles of justice proposed by John Rawls in *A Theory of Justice* (Cambridge, MA: Harvard University Press, 1971).

66. Sen, *The Idea of Justice*, 57.

67. Sen, 12

68. Beckert, *Inherited Wealth*, 198-203.

69. Guido Erreygers and Toon Vendevelde, eds., *Is Inheritance Legitimate? Ethical and Economic Aspects of Wealth Transfers* (New York: Springer, 1997), 25, 27, 141.

70. Beckert, *Inherited Wealth*, 178.

71. Cunliffe and Erreygers, *Is Inheritance Legitimate?* 3

72. Erreygers and Vendevelde, 35; see also Chester, *Inheritance, Wealth, and Society*, 28-30.

73. Erreygers and Vandevelde, 46, 151.

74. Erreygers and Vendevelde, 33.

75. In the United States, gifts to spouses and to charities are exempt from federal estate tax. The taxable estate is thus net of these gifts. Taking the tax "off the top" of the net estate before assets are distributed to the rest of the beneficiaries impacts all of them equally. In contrast, inheritance taxes reduce the amount that each beneficiary receives to different degrees depending on the closeness of the relationship to the deceased (the closer the relationship, the lower the tax rate).

76. Pierre Pestieau, *The Role of Gift and Estate Transfers in the United States and Europe*, www.crepp.ulg.ac.be/papers/crepp-wp200202.pfd, 3.

77. Atkinson, *Inequality: What Can Be Done?* 237-8.

78. Atkinson, 194. In another of his ten proposals, Atkinson says that revenue from this lifetime tax could be used to finance an inequality-reducing minimum inheritance for everyone. "There should be a capital endowment (minimum inheritance) paid to all in [early] adulthood."

79. Andrew Chamberlain, "Poll Questions on the Estate Tax," Taxfoundation.org/blog/poll-questions-estate-tax.

80. American Bar Association, *Guide to Wills and Estates: Everything You Need to Know About Wills, Estates, Trusts, and Taxes* (New York: Random House, 2012), 236-237. State estate taxes are collected in Connecticut, Delaware, Hawaii, Illinois, Maine, Massachusetts, Minnesota, New York, Oregon, Rhode Island, Vermont, Washington and the District of Columbia; inheritance taxes in Iowa, Kentucky, Nebraska and Pennsylvania; and both taxes in Maryland and New Jersey. Tax rates vary. See Morgan Scarboro, "Does Your State Have an Estate or Inheritance Tax?" https://taxfoundation.org/state-inheritance-tax, May 25, 2017.

81. Karlyn Bowman, "A Killer Tax," *Forbes Online*, December 7, 2009.

82. Jordan Weissmann, "How to Make Americans Love the Death Tax," http://www.slate.com/blogs/moneybox/2015/03/27/the_estate_tax_here_s_how_to_make_americans_love_it.html.

83. Shammas, Salmon and Dahlin, *Inheritance in America.*

84. Thomas Piketty and Gabriel Zucman, "Wealth and Inheritance in the Long Run," *Handbook of Income Distribution, Volume 2B* (Elsevier, 2015), 1326 (emphasis added).

85. Cunliffe and Erreygers, *Inherited Wealth, Justice, and Equality*, 77-9.

86. Shammas, Salmon and Dahlin, *Inheritance in America*, 144.

87. Miller and McNamee, *Inheritance and Wealth in America*, 76. For a comprehensive review see Michael J. Graetz and Ian Shapiro, *Death by a Thousand Cuts: The Fight over Taxing Inherited Wealth* (Princeton University Press, 2005).

88. Jeanne Sahadi, "New estate tax law gives an enormous gift to rich families." *CNNMoney*, January 9, 2018. money.cnn.com/2018/01/09/pf/taxes/estate-tax/index.html.

89. Miller and McNamee, *Inheritance and Wealth in America*, 5; see also Beckert, *Inherited Wealth*, 2013.

90. In November of 2016, Donald Trump proposed the complete elimina-
tion of the federal estate tax, thus paving the way for what reporter
Paul Sullivan called "A Wider Path to Dynastic Wealth," *New York Times*,
November 12, 2016. The doubling of exemptions in December 2017
accomplished almost as much, with fewer than 1,800 estates expected
to be taxable under the new rules in 2018 (Sahadi, "New estate tax
laws").

91. Pierre Pestieau, *The Role of Gift and Estate Transfers in the United States
and Europe*, www.crepp.ulg.ac.be/papers/crepp-wp200202.pfd,
33; Cunliffe and Erreygers, *Inherited Wealth, Justice, and Equality* 5;
Atkinson, *Inequality: What Can Be Done?* 179, 193.

92. Beckert, *Inherited Wealth*, 169.

93. Nicholas Fitz, "Economic Inequality: It's Far Worse Than You Think."
Scientific American, March 31, 2015.

94. Jordan Weissman, "How to Make Americans Love the Death Tax."

95. Fitz, "Economic Inequality: It's Far Worse Than You Think."

96. Emmanuel Saez and Gabriel Zucman, "Exploding wealth inequality in the United States" (Washington Center for Equitable Growth,
2014), 1.

97. Fitz, "Economic Inequality: It's Far Worse Than You Think." A
report from Pew Research Center explains that Americans on
the whole don't resent the fact that some people are very rich
(although they do feel that the wealthy don't pay their fair share
in taxes). Rather, "they just want a better chance of achieving success themselves" and would like to see government policies "that
give everyone a fair shot." See "For the Public, It's Not About Class
Warfare, But Fairness," http://www.people-press/org/2012/03/02/
for-the-public-its-not-about-class-warfare-but-fairness/.

98. Section headings in Clifford, *Plan Your Estate* (nine of 32 chapters) and American Bar Association, *Guide to Wills and Estates* (three of 29 chapters).

99. Miller and McNamee, *Inheritance and Wealth in America*, 1-2.

100. Atkinson, *Inequality: What Can Be Done?* 11.

Chapter Three

101. Cynthia D'Aprix Sweeney, *The Nest. A Novel* (New York: Harper Collins), 31 (emphasis added).

102. MetLife, *The Metlife Study of Inheritance and Wealth Transfer to Baby Boomers* (New York: MetLife Mature Market Institute, 2010), 13.

103. Cunliffe and Erreygers, *Inherited Wealth, Justice and Equality*, 1.

104. *The MetLife Study*, 2-3.

105. Tami Luhby, "Wealth inequality between blacks and whites worsens," money.cnn.com/2013/02/27/news/economy/wealth-whites-blacks/.

106. Nicholas Fitz, "Economic Inequality: It's Far Worse Than You Think."

107. An Ohio study found that 38 percent of heirs (most of whom were over sixty at the time they inherited) saved the money they received. Twenty-five percent used it for living expenses, 16 percent bought real estate, 8 percent paid bills, another 8 percent made purchases, 4 percent used it for education and 2 percent for a vacation. A few made charitable gifts. Sussman, Cates and Smith, *The Family and Inheritance*, 154,161.

108. Jay L. Zagorsky, "Do people save or spend their inheritances? Understanding what happens to inherited wealth," *Journal of Family and Economic Issues* 34, 1 (2013), 71-72. Relatively few had inherited

anything so far, however (most of their parents were still living) and the amounts received were low as well (median $11,340, mean $52,474).

109. *The MetLife Study*, 16.

110. Elizabeth R. Carter, "Tipping the Scales in Favor of Charitable Bequests: A Critique," *Pace Law Review* 34 (2014), 983.

111. Kyunmin Kim et al., "Agreement between aging parent's bequest intention and middle-aged child's inheritance expectation," *Gerontologist* 53 (2013).

112. Richard E. Barnes, *Estate Planning for Blended Families*; Denis Clifford, *Plan Your Estate*; Sally Balch Hurme's *Checklist for My Family* (AARP and American Bar Association, 2015).

113. American Bar Association, *Guide to Wills and Estates*, 67.

114. Heirs are not personally responsible for paying debts of the deceased unless they have co-signed or otherwise guaranteed a loan. (Spouses in community property states are liable for community debts, however.) But executors are obligated to pay taxes and administrative expenses before distributing whatever remains to the beneficiaries.

115. Clifford, *Plan Your Estate*, 39-40.

116. Nine states have community property systems: Arizona, California, Idaho, Nevada, New Mexico, Texas, and Washington; Wisconsin's system is called "marital property." Two are mixed: couples living in Alaska and Tennessee may opt for community property with a written agreement. Property arrangements of all other states and the District of Columbia are based on English common law except for Louisiana, which is based on the Napoleonic Code.

117. Clifford, *Plan Your Estate*, 47. See Frederick Hertz, Ralph Warner and Toni Ihara for information on *Living Together: A Legal Guide for Unmarried Couples* (Nolo, 2013).

118. Nolo, "Marriage and Property Ownership: Who Owns What?" www.nolo.com/legal-encyclopedia/marriage-property-owner-ship-who-owns-what-29841.html. See also National Conference of Commissioners on Uniform State Laws, *Uniform Probate Code*, "Marital Property Based on Different Theories of Partnership," 79.

119. American Bar Association, *Guide to Wills and Estates*, 61.

120. Accettura, *Blood & Money*, 216 (emphasis added).

121. Revisions to the Uniform Probate Code (last updated February 11, 2013) of the National Conference of Commissioners on Uniform State Laws leave larger shares to the surviving spouse than previously. For example, "If the decedent leaves no surviving descendants and no surviving parent, or if the decedent does leave surviving descendants but neither the decedent nor the surviving spouse has other descendants, the surviving spouse is entitled to all of the decedent's intestate estate. However, "if the decedent leaves no surviving descendants but does leave a surviving parent, the decedent's surviving spouse receives the first $300,000 plus three-fourths of the balance of the intestate estate" (National Conference of Commissioners on Uniform State Laws, 30-31).

122. American Bar Association, *Plan Your Estate*, 233. Exemptions do not apply to property left to noncitizen spouses, however.

123. Shammas, Salmon and Dahlin, *Inheritance in America*, 16.

124. Shammas, Salmon and Dahlin, 184.

125. Angel, *Inheritance in Contemporary America*, 21.

126. Alison Aughinbaugh, Omar Robles and Hugette Sun, "Marriage and divorce: patterns by gender, race, and educational attainment," *Monthly Labor Review* 32 (October 2013), Table 3.

127. Jane Bryant Quinn, "Divorce Will Cost You," www.aarp.org/money/investing/info-2014/divorce-will-cost-you.html.

128. Sussman, Cates and Smith, *The Family and Inheritance*, 147.

129. Barnes, *Estate Planning for Blended Families*, 117.

130. American Bar Association, *Guide to Wills and Estates*, 155; Clifford, *Plan Your Estate*, 371.

131. Accettura, *Blood & Money*, 40.

132. www.socialsecurity.gov/OACT/population/longevity.html.

133. Vanguard, "Plan for a long retirement," https://personal/vanguard.com/us/insights/retirement/plan-for-a-long-retirement.

134. Life expectancies of fifty-year-old men in the lowest-income fifth of all households have risen in over the past three decades from about seventy-seven to eighty-two years, for example, and of fifty-year-old women from eighty-two to eight-six years—that is, about three to four years on average. But in the highest-income fifth, men's life expectancies at age fifty have risen from seventy-six to eighty-nine and women's from seventy-eight to ninety-two—an extra thirteen or fourteen years of life. National Academies of Sciences, Engineering, and Medicine, *The Growing Gap in Life Expectancy by Income: Implications for Federal Programs and Policy Responses* (Washington, DC: National Academies Press), 52.

135. AARP Health Care Costs Calculator, www.aarp.org/work/retirement-planning/the-aarp-healthcare-costs-calculator.html.

136. Christina Hoff Sommers, "Filial Morality," in *Women and Moral Theory*, ed. Eva Feder Kittay and Diana T. Meyers (Totowa, NJ: Rowman & Littlefield, 1987), 69-70.

137. Shammas, Salmon and Dahlin, *Inheritance in America*, 160. By 2014, 5 percent of women and men sixty-five and older were living in households with a grandchild present, perhaps slightly more with adult children. United States Department of Health and Human Services, *A Profile of Older Americans: 2014*, 5.

138. Jeffrey Blustein, *Parents and Children: The Ethics of the Family* (Oxford University Press, 1982), 71-78.

139. Katherine C. Pearson, "Filial support laws in the modern era." This is not to say that adult children do not by and large feel responsible for providing at least some aspects of parental care if needed. One survey found that 83 percent of adult respondents said they would feel "very obligated" to assist a parent who needed either financial help or caregiving, for example, and 56 percent to a stepparent (Pew Research Center, "A Portrait of Stepfamilies," January 13, 2011).

140. Shammas, Salmon and Dahlin, *Inheritance in America*, 160.

141. Accettura, *Blood & Money*, 206-7

142. Accettura, *Blood & Money*, 235.

143. American Bar Association, "Estate taxes," 232-248. Surviving spouses can claim the unused portion of the exemption for their estates as well as their own allotment. Transfers for tuition or medical care do not count as gifts as long as they are made directly to the provider and not to the individual beneficiary.

144. Leonard's offspring in Cynthia Sweeney's novel are counting on their nest eggs, little realizing (spoiler warning) that collusion between the trustee and one sibling would make it disappear.

145. Fabian R. Pfeffer and Robert F. Schoeni, "How Inequality Shapes Our Future," *The Russell Sage Foundation Journal of the Social Sciences*, 2, 1 (2016), 2-22

146. Sussman, Cates and Smith, *The Family and Inheritance*, 6.

147. More than three-quarters of all U.S. households with "heads" age sixty-five or older own a home; the same proportion own income-earning assets in a financial institution. One-third have IRA or KEOGH accounts; one-quarter own stocks and mutual fund shares; one-fifth own 401K or thrift savings plans. Between 5 and 10 percent of older households own savings bonds, equity in a business or profession, rental property, other real estate, and/or other income-earning assets. United States Census Bureau, "Net worth and asset ownership

of households: 2011," http://www.census.gov/people/wealth/, Tables 1, 2.

148. Maria Vornovitsky et al., "Distribution of Household Wealth in the U.S.: 2000 to 2011," United States Census Bureau (2014), Table A1.

149. United States Census Bureau, "Net worth and asset ownership of households: 2011," http://www.census.gov/people/wealth/, Table 1. In a slightly different formulation, a 2013 national Survey of Consumer Finances conducted by the Federal Reserve Board reports on the net worth of *families* within households, which they describe as the "primary economic unit" of a single person or couple plus other related and financially interdependent persons within the household (Jesse Bricker et al., "Changes in U.S. family finances from 2010 to 2013"). The median net worth of families in this survey with heads aged 65-74 is $232,100—considerably higher than the U.S. census survey—and the mean is $1,057.000, the latter reflecting a strong upward pull on the arithmetic average by the very rich. Among families with heads aged 75 and older, the median drops to $194,80 and the mean $645,200 as the "primary economic unit" shifts to one-person households.

150. Anne Warren, "Choosing the Objects of Your Bounty: Estate Planning for Unmarried Individuals and Individuals Without Children," *Philanthropy and Wealth Planning* (December 5, 2016). Although this article is addressed to testators without a spouse or offspring, Warren's advice on making lifetime gifts and other matters is highly relevant to everyone.

151. Some critics contend that public policies favoring testamentary bequests to non-profit organizations with tax write-offs compete unfairly with the welfare of surviving spouses and children. "Testamentary bequests play an important role in the financial plans of non-profit organizations," says law professor Elizabeth Carter. "Many...are looking...to the Baby Boomer wealth transfer as an important source of funding."

With gifts from wills and trusts amounting to an estimated 8 percent of total annual charitable giving, Carter claims that aggressive solicitations could result in the "potential exploitation of testators and their families by the nonprofit sector" (Carter, "Tipping the Scales," 1019).

152. Martha Britton Eller, "Charitable bequests: evidence from federal estate tax returns." https://www.irs.gov/pub/irs-soi/95eschar.pdf, 183.

153. Eller, 178-9.

154. In the Ohio study of probate wills, only 25 of 422 sampled wills included a charitable bequest, most often to a church. Most gifts were small, made in addition to family bequests. Testators with no immediate family and those with larger estates were more likely to leave to charity (Sussman, Cates and Smith, *The Family and Inheritance*, 115-117).

Chapter Four

155. Angel, *Inheritance in Contemporary America*, 85.

156. Angel, 83

157. Accettura, *Blood & Money*, 70-3.

158. Accettura, *Blood & Money*, 249.

159. Velasquez et al., "Justice and Fairness."

160. Pew Research Center, "A Portrait of Stepfamilies," January 13, 2011.

161. Barnes, *Estate Planning for Blended Families*, 156.

162. A twice-divorced mother of a son and daughter by different fathers describes her dilemma. "David's going to get a big inheritance from Sam and Sam's mother. Emma got hers already when her dad died last year: ten thousand dollars. He had a new family, you know, and he never did earn much. I'm giving them equal shares. Who knows how Emma's life will turn out? David has agreed that he'll help Emma out if she ever needs it. What else could I do?" (personal communication).

163. The same argument could be made of grandchildren and of nieces and nephews, as long as they are of the same generation and degree of relationship to the testator.

164. Angel, *Inheritance in Contemporary America*, 85 (emphasis added). Despite this summary statement, Angel does describe some ethnic differences in parental support for children through *inter vivos* gifts and inheritance (40-50, 85). A five-state survey inquiring about hypothetical decisions people would make in their wills elicited a number of normative preferences, including this one: "all [biological] children [in the same generation should] share equally in the estate, regardless of whether they were born of different marriages or whether they are legitimate or nonmarital children" (Fellows, Simon, and Rau, "Public attitudes about property distribution at death and intestate succession laws in the United States," 387).

165. Henry Klosowski, "The hazards of unequal inheritance," *Wall Street Journal*, August 26, 2014.

166. Rawls, *Justice as Fairness*, 55-58.

167. Velasquez et al., "Justice and Fairness."

168. Barnes, *Estate Planning for Blended Families*, 40.

169. Audrey Light and Kathleeen McGarry, "Why Parents Play Favorites: Explanations for Unequal Bequests" (Cambridge, MA: National Bureau of Economic Research, 2003), 23-24.

170. Light and McGarry, 25.

171. Anthony Atkinson makes this observation when he asks, "What accounts for unequal outcomes even in the face of equal opportunity?" in *Inequality: What Can Be Done?* 10-11.

172. What's interesting about this inequity from the perspective of the concentration of wealth is that better-educated and higher-earning adults tend to have fewer children than those who are less well off. There has also has been a shift toward higher-earning men and women (e.g.,

two professionals) marrying one another, which doubly compounds the unequal distribution of incomes and assets across households (Atkinson, *Inequality: What Can Be Done?* 158-160).

173. National Conference of Commissioners on Uniform State Laws, Uniform Probate Code, Section 2-109.

174. A case in point: Beth's father paid for four years of special education for her son with learning disabilities, which she couldn't afford as a single mom. Beth's siblings claimed that the entire amount should be subtracted from her share of their father's estate. With nothing except the accounts her father kept of monthly payments for his grandson's tuition, Beth successfully claimed that this was a gift to the boy and not a loan to her (personal communication).

175. Quoctrung Bui, "Almost Half of Young Adults Get Rent Help From Parents," *New York Times*, February 9, 2017.

176. Pfeffer and Schoeni, "How Wealth Inequality Shapes Our Future." "Transfers received from parents for schooling are more than eleven times larger among children whose parents are in the top quarter of the wealth distribution compared to children from the bottom *half*" (emphasis added).

177. Light and McGarry, "Why Parents Play Favorites."

178. Thomas A. Dunn and John W. Phillips, "The timing and division of parental transfers to children," *Economics Letters* 54 (1997).

179. Dunn and Phillips, 135.

180. https://www.lectlaw.com/files/cur07.htm.

181. Velasqez et al., 1 (emphasis added).

182. Sussman, Cates, and Smith, *The Family and Inheritance*, 212.

183. Blustein, *Parents and Children*, 71.

184. Blustein, 76.

185. Light and McGarry, "Why Parents Play Favorites," 25.

186. Light and McGarry, 23-24.

187. Stepler, "5 facts about family caregivers."

188. Angel, *Inheritance in Contemporary America*, 40.

189. Jane Smiley, *A Thousand Acres* (New York: Ivy Books, 1991), 19. "Well Ginny," says attorney Ken LaSalle on p. 259, " Your dad is suing you to get the farm back. Your sister Caroline is a party to the suit, too. You better find yourself a lawyer."

190. Robert H. Mnookin, *Bargaining with the Devil: When to Negotiate, When to Fight* (Simon and Schuster Paperbacks, 2010), 232.

191. Remi P. Clignet, "Ethnicity and inheritance," in *Inheritance and Wealth in America*, eds. Robert K. Miller Jr. and Stephen J. McNamee (New York: Plenum Press, 1998), 127-129; see also Simone Wegge, "Inheritance Systems, " in *Oxford Encyclopedia of Economic History*, ed. Joel Mokyr (Oxford University Press, 2003), 77-83.

192. Accettura, *Blood & Money*, 226.

193. Clignet, "Ethnicity and inheritance," 127.

194. Ivette Santaella, personal communication, www.blackwellsantaellalaw.com.

Chapter Five

195. Marlene S. Stum, "'I Just Want to be Fair': Interpersonal Justice in Intergenerational Transfers of Non-Titled Property," *Family Relations* 48 (1999), 159.

196. American Bar Association, *Guide to Wills and Estates*, "Sample Basic Will," 368.

197. Will of Benjamin Franklin, www.livingtrustnetwork.com. His gift was not without conditions, however. He asked that his daughter "would not form any of those diamonds into ornaments either for herself or [her own] daughters, and thereby introduce or countenance the expensive, vain, and useless fashion of wearing jewels in this country."

198. Will of Thomas Jefferson, www.livingtrustnetwork.com.

199. An aggrieved claimant may challenge the terms of the will in court, although success is unlikely and costs will soar. On the positive side, heirs may redistribute what they receive in order to make things right. In the Ohio study, 50 of the heirs among 360 testate cases in which survivors were interviewed had redistributed items such as a car, furniture, jewelry, or even who got the house, sometimes including a disinherited sibling. Half of the 147 intestate cases with survivor interviews involved some redistribution. Not all is predictable: where the distribution was unequal, many thought it should have been equal, and vice versa (Sussman, Cates and Smith, *The Family and Inheritance*, 121-148).

200. American Bar Association, *Guide to Wills and Estates*, 307; Barnes, *Estate Planning for Blended Families*, 200-202; Julie Hall, *How to Divide Your Family's Estate and Heirlooms Peacefully & Sensibly* (Charlotte, NC: The Estate Lady Publications, 2010), 24. See also Mary Randolph, *The Executor's Guide: Settling a Loved One's Estate or Trust* (Berkeley, CA: Nolo, 2016).

201. Hall, "How to Divide Your Family's Estate," p 84. "Avoid selecting one or more children as trustees/executors," advises attorney Paula Leibovitz Goodwin, "unless you are absolutely certain that they get along and can work things out. The worst thing to do is to name them as co-trustees" (personal communication).

202. Jeffrey P. Rosenfeld, "Will Contests," in Miller and McNamee, *Inheritance and Wealth in America*, 177-179. Litigation is rare and expensive, and more likely to be unsuccessful than not. In one sample of over seven thousand wills, fewer than 1 percent were contested.

203. Stum, "I Just Want to be Fair," 159.

204. Sen, *The Idea of Justice*, 17.

205. Martha C. Nussbaum, *Political Emotions: Why Love Matters for Justice* (Cambridge, MA: Belknap Press, 2015), 22 (emphasis added).

206. Eva Feder Kittay and Diana T. Meyers, "Introduction," in Kittay and Meyers, *Women and Moral Theory*, 7 (emphasis added).

207. Carol Gilligan, "Moral orientation and moral development," in Kittay and Meyers, *Women and Moral Theory*, 24.

208. Stum, "I Just Want to be Fair," 162.

209. Stum, 162.

210. Hall, "How to Divide Your Family's Estate," 15, 22,

211. Hall, 20 (emphasis added).

212. Hall, 41.

213. Leibovitz Goodwin, personal communication, https://www.perkins-coie.com/en/professionals/paula-leibovitz-goodwin.html.

214. Stum, "I Just Want to be Fair," 164.

Chapter Six

215. Kittay and Meyers, *Women and Moral Theory*, "Introduction," 11.

216. Lori R. Sackler with Todd Gutner, *The M Word: The Money Talk Every Family Needs to Have About Wealth and Their Financial Future* (New York: McGraw Hill, 2013): 19.

217. Marlene S. Stum, "Family and inheritance decisions: examining non-titled property transfers," *Journal of Family and Economic Issues*, 21 (2000): 185.

218. UBS Investor Watch Report, "Begin before the end: Why families need to have inheritance conversations now" (UBS Investor Watch 3Q, 2014). The sample consists of men and women ages 21-36 ("Millennials") and older investors. All have $250,000 or more investable income (excluding value of their homes); half have $1 million or more.

219. UBS, "Begin before the end," 11.

220. Accettura, *Blood & Money*, 201-202.

221. Jane Bryant Quinn, "'The Talk': Your Kids and Your Money," www.aarp.org/money/budgeting-saving/info-2015/talking-to-kids-about-money.html.

222. Sackler, *The M Word*, 78.

223. Dan Fitzgerald, quoted in Quinn, "The Talk," 1.

224. Barnes, *Estate Planning for Blended Families*, 282-302.

225. John Gromala, "Estate planning: a preemptive strike against potential litigation." www.mediate.com/articles/estate.cfm.

226. Deborah Tannen, *You Just Don't Understand: Women and Men in Conversation* (Ballantine Books, 1991).

227. Mnookin, *Bargaining With the Devil*, 235.

228. Janet E. Taylor and Joan E. Norris, "Sibling Relationships, Fairness, and Conflict Over Transfer of the Farm," *Family Relations* 49 (2000): 277.

229. Sackler, *The M Word*, 89; see also Clifford, *Plan Your Estate*, 430-440.

230. Nancy L. Powers, personal communication, PowersLaw@aol.com.

231. Expression borrowed from *ToughConversations.net*.

232. Sig Cohen and Carolyn Miller Parr, *ToughConversations.net*.

233. Gromola, "Estate planning: a preemptive strike," www.mediate.com/articles/estate.cfm.

234. Powers, personal communication. See also Nancy L. Powers, "The Best Estate Plan is No Match for Unprepared Heirs," *Wealth Counsel Quarterly* 6, 4 (October 2012), 1-2.

235. Mnookin, *Bargaining With the Devil*, 247.

236. For example, John Gromala: "The mediator confers, on a confidential basis, with each person separately and with the parties jointly."

237. Mnookin, *Bargaining With the Devil*, 237.

238. Roger Fisher and William Uris with Bruce Patton, ed., *Getting to Yes: Negotiating Agreement Without Giving In* (Penguin Books, 2011).

239. Fisher and Uris, *Getting to Yes*, 155-8 (emphasis added).

240. Jan Frankel Schau and Nina Meirding, "Negotiating Like a Woman – How Gender Impacts Communication between the Sexes," www.mediate.com/articles/ShauMeierding.cfm.

241. Marshall Whitley, "Enough About Avoiding Probate...Let's Avoid Probate Litigation!" http://digitalcommons.law.ggu.edu/cgi/viewcontent.cgi?article=1785&context=pubs.

242. Clifford, *Plan Your Estate*, 454.

243. Chapter checklists can be downloaded, filled out, saved and printed.

244. Tina Kreitz, *The Last Gift Box: A Present to Those Who Follow Me*, Lastgiftbox.com.

245. Kreitz, 34, 36.

246. Elizabeth Arnold, *Creating the Good Will* (Portfolio, 2001).

247. Malcolm, *Two* Lives, 201-202, as quoted in the Introduction.

248. Genesis 49:1, 28, 29, 33 (King James version of the Bible).

GLOSSARY

A brief walk in the woods of some legal terminology

Definitions of legal terms can be found on-line and in many publications on estate planning. The following are adapted solely for this book and are not intended for legal purposes.

Assets are tangible or intangible items of economic value that we own, such as a house or condo, vacation home, vehicles, personal and household effects, cash deposits, pensions, retirement accounts, life insurance policies, business shares and investments (see property). As described in Chapter Three for American households, our **net assets** (**net worth**) are the total value of our assets minus our debts (mortgages, car payments, credit card balances, etc.)

Beneficiary is a person or organization named to receive benefits from a particular gift or contract, such as a trust, will, bank account, retirement account or insurance policy.

Bequest as narrowly defined is a gift of personal property (usually other than money) made (bequeathed) to a specified person or organization named in a will or trust. More generally, a bequest refers to any gift of property made by means of a will or trust including real estate (otherwise known as a **devise**) and money (a **legacy**).

Charity as defined here is a non-profit organization with a religious, humanitarian, educational, scientific, or other beneficial purpose. Cash or in-kind contributions given to qualified charitable organizations while the testator is alive, or in a will or trust, are tax deductible.

Common law is a body of law that has evolved from a combination of custom, usage and court decisions. As noted in Chapter One, the legal system of the United States is based largely on English common law that has been adapted, expanded and codified over the years by state statutes.

Common law marriage is a legally recognized marital category in some states for persons who have lived together for many years and represent themselves as a married couple.

Estate is all of the property or assets we own as individuals at the time of our death, no matter how little: our home and other real estate (depending on the title) and our personal property. Insurance, pensions, real estate, vehicles, personal belongings, and debts are all part of our estate (see assets).

Estate planning is the act of preparing for the transfer of our assets after our death. Among other things, we document our financial assets and liabilities; select guardians (for minor children) and executors (of a will) or trustees (of a trust); and prepare powers of attorney. A process of *participatory estate planning* involving family members is described in Chapter Six.

Estate taxes are levied by the federal and some state governments on the total value of the assets we own and plan to pass on at our death after debts are paid and exemptions are calculated (e.g., spousal transfers and charitable contributions). Estate taxes are paid *before* the remainder is passed on to the designated heirs. The minimal thresholds for taxation as well as the tax rates vary by state. The value of the **gross estate**—the total property owned at the time of death regardless of debts or liens—determines whether an estate must file a federal tax return. Taxes are levied on the value of the **net estate** plus the value of taxable gifts made during the three years preceding death (see gift taxes).

Executor is a person or institution (such as a bank or trust company) named in a will as the testator's personal representative to administer the estate (assemble property, pay debts and taxes, make distributions, etc.) and carry out other wishes of the deceased as described in Chapter Five. A **fiduciary** is a person or company appointed by the testator to act as executor of a will or trustee of a trust.

Gifts are transfers of valuable personal property such as cash, stocks and bonds, art works, heirlooms, jewelry, etc. from one person to another made during the donor's lifetime (**inter vivos**). Major gifts made by the deceased "in anticipation of death" (**causa mortis**) within the last three years of life are counted as part of the estate for federal tax purposes. **Gift taxes** are levied by the federal government on gifts we make to other individuals, including our children, during our lifetime. Officially called the unified gift and estate tax, the tax applies to property that is given away during life or at death. Most gifts made during life are exempt from the tax, including gifts of up to $15,000 per year per recipient (beginning in 2018, up from $14,000 from 2013 to 2017), gifts to tax-exempt charities, gifts to a spouse, and gifts made for tuition or medical bills. Beginning in 2018, any person can give away or leave at death a total of almost $11 million free of the gift and estate tax (double the amount of 2017). The tax is assessed at death unless we give away more than the exempt amount in taxable gifts during our life.

Health Care Advance Directive is a legal document in which we declare our wishes for the type of medical treatment we want to receive (or not), especially toward the end of our life, and name a person (agent) who is responsible for making sure our wishes are carried out (see power of attorney).

Inheritance as narrowly defined refers to property we receive upon the death of a relative resulting from the laws of descent and distribution. More generally, it refers to any property received upon the death of someone, regardless of the relationship. These distinctions parallel those of an **heir,** a person who is legally entitled under state law to inherit from the deceased as a close family member, and an **inheritor,** a person or organization who receives property from any deceased person's estate. **Inheritance taxes** are imposed by some states (but not the federal government) on the value of property that an inheritor receives from the deceased. Inheritances received by the spouse or children of the deceased are usually not taxed. The more distant the relationship, the higher the tax on that person's inheritance is likely to be.

Last Will and Testament is a document stating who is to inherit our property, administer the estate, and other details (see will). It used to be that a **will** was designed to distribute (**devise**) real property and a **testament** to make gifts of (**bequeath**) personal property through separate arrangements. The distinction persists in Thomas Jefferson's will in Chapter One in which he writes, "I do hereby devise and bequeath all the residue of my property real and personal ..."

Power of attorney is a legal document made and signed by the grantor, or principle, that grants to a specific person the legal right to act on his or her behalf in general, or regarding specific decisions. A **durable power of attorney** remains in effect even if the grantor becomes incapacitated. A **power of attorney for finances** grants to a specific person the authority to manage our financial affairs if we become incapacitated, whereas a **power of attorney for health care** grants a specific person permission to make medical decisions on our behalf if are unable to make these decisions ourselves (see *health care advance directive*).

Probate is the legal process by which the courts review a will to determine whether it is valid and authentic. Probate also refers to the court administration of the will of the deceased or the estate of a person who dies without a will. Property placed in joint tenancy, a living trust, or a "pay-on-death account" (e.g., bank account or life insurance policy with a specified beneficiary) does not go through probate because it is not part of a will. Probate Court is part of the state judicial system charged primarily with handling wills and estates as well as conservatorships and guardianships of those who are not mentally competent to manage their own affairs.

Property includes everything that we own as individuals of whatever monetary or sentimental value, including real and personal property (see assets). **Real property** (also known as real estate, or realty) refers to land and any buildings and other immovable structures that are fixed permanently to the land as well natural resources such as oil, gas and timber, any improvements that have been made to the land (wells, roads, etc.), and any rights and interests in the land. **Personal property** (also quaintly known as chattels, or personalty) consists of our movable possessions, that is, anything but real estate that is left under the terms of a will.

These personal possessions may be **tangible** ("touchable") items such as livestock, tools and equipment, merchandise, household goods and furnishings, clothing and jewelry, antiques, art works, photographs, automobiles and boats, and special collections, or **intangible** items such as stocks, bonds, bank accounts, intellectual property, "good-will value," and so on.

Marital property is property that is owned by both spouses according to the laws of each state. In **community property** states, property acquired and income earned by either spouse after marriage (and before a permanent separation) and debts incurred by either spouse during the marriage generally accrue to both spouses equally as community or marital property, regardless of whose name is on the title. Property that either spouse owned before the marriage or receives by inheritance, gift, or as the profits from property owned before marriage remains **separate property** unless it is comingled with the community or contractually agreed. Community property laws exist in Arizona, California, Idaho, Nevada, New Mexico, Texas, Washington, and Wisconsin. In Alaska, couples can create community property by written agreement. In **non community property (common law)** states, whether property is considered marital or separate depends primarily on how it is titled (see the discussion of "What do we really *own* in a marriage?" in Chapter Three).

Property ownership: whether we can pass on property in our will depends on whether we actually own it, or a share of it, in our own right. In the case of real estate or some other types of property, this depends on the legal status of our ownership (or tenancy). In **joint tenancy**, two or more people share ownership as joint tenants. When one joint tenant dies, the others automatically acquire the deceased owner's share by right of survivorship. The deceased tenant's share does not become part of his or her will. With **tenancy in common,** two or more people share ownership as tenants in common. When one owner dies, the deceased owner's share passes to his or her heirs through a personal will or trust.

Testator is a person who makes and signs a will providing for the disposition of his or her property after death. A person who leaves a valid will dies **testate**; one without dies **intestate.** Intestacy cases are referred to probate court, which appoints an administrator to distribute the estate according to state statutes. These include rules of **intestate succession** that determine how property must be distributed among the closest surviving relatives. As described in Chapter One, **testamentary freedom** refers to the act of making a will in which we choose our beneficiaries according to our personal preferences. **Testamentary capacity** means having the mental competency to execute a will.

Trust: Nolo's legal dictionary defines a trust as follows (*www.nolo.com/dictionary*):

> An arrangement under which one person, a trustee, manages property for a beneficiary. The person who creates the trust is called the settlor, trustor, or grantor. There are many kinds of trusts, some created during the settlor's lifetime and some at death. Trusts are used for, among other things, avoiding probate court proceedings, saving on estate tax, providing quality management of assets, and keeping money out of the hands of improvident beneficiaries.

Revocable trusts (living trusts) are often recommended as a method of avoiding the costs and delays of a will passing through probate. The **trustee** sets up the trust while he or she is still alive and controls it until death, at which time the designated **successor trustee** distributes the assets directly to beneficiaries named in the trust. The original trustee places all titled assets in the name of the trust and prepares a will naming the trust as beneficiary of the residue of the estate. **Irrevocable trusts (permanent trusts)** are exactly that, designed to pass down unchanged through the generations. They bear an eerie resemblance to the English entails described for Downton Abbey in Chapter One.

Bypass Trusts are set up for the immediate benefit of a surviving spouse who may draw on the income from the trust until his or her death, at which point it passes to the children, grandchildren, or other beneficiaries. **Generation-skipping trusts** permit the originator's adult child to draw on the trust income until death, at which point it passes to the grandchildren. Both of these arrangements are designed to avoid estate taxes. **Spendthrift trusts** rely on an appointed trustee to parcel out the flow of money to a possibly reckless beneficiary and to pay the beneficiary's creditors directly from the trust if needed.

Will (see Last Will and Testament) is a legal document in which we state who is to inherit our property, who is to execute the will, how to pay our debts and taxes, and (if needed) who should be a guardian of our minor children, among other things. To be valid, it must be signed by the maker (the *testator*), dated, and witnessed by two people. Some states will accept a **holographic will** that is handwritten in its entirety and also signed and witnessed. A **codicil** is an amendment made to a will in a separate written document that modifies or partially revokes an existing or earlier will. As is the case for the will itself, the testator must sign the codicil in front of witnesses (and be of sound mind, etc.). Finally, a **contested will** is one that is challenged in court on specific grounds by the survivors of the deceased or their legal representatives. This is what we try to avoid by being fair in the first place and, if we wish, by engaging in participatory estate planning with family members (see Chapter Six).

BIBLIOGRAPHY

Accettura, P. Mark. *Blood & Money: Why Families Fight Over Inheritance and What to Do About It.* Farmington Hills MI: Collinwood Press, 2011.

Alston, Lee J., and Morton Owen Schapiro. "Inheritance laws across colonies: causes and consequences." *Journal of Economic History* 44, 2 (1984): 277-287.

American Bar Association. *Guide to Wills and Estates: Everything You Need to Know About Wills, Estates, Trusts, and Taxes* (Fourth edition). New York: Random House, 2012.

Angel, Jacqueline L. *Inheritance in Contemporary America: The Social Dimensions of Giving Across Generations.* Baltimore: Johns Hopkins University Press, 2008.

Arnold, Elizabeth. *Creating the Good Will: The Most Comprehensive Guide to Both the Financial and Emotional Sides of Passing On Your Legacy.* Portfolio Reprint Edition, 2006.

Atkinson, Anthony B. *Inequality: What Can Be Done?* Cambridge MA: Harvard University Press, 2015.

Aughinbaugh, Alison, Omar Robles, and Hugette Sun. "Marriage and divorce: patterns by gender, race, and educational attainment," *Monthly Labor Review,* U.S. Bureau of Labor Statistics, October 2013. https://doi.org/10.219/mlr.2013.32.

Barnes, Richard E. *Estate Planning for Blended Families: Providing for your Spouse & Children in a Second Marriage.* Berkeley CA: Nolo, 2009.

Bean, J. M. W. *The Decline of English Feudalism, 1215-1540.* Manchester University Press, 1968.

Beckert, Jens. *Inherited Wealth.* Princeton NJ: Princeton University Press, 2008.

Blustein, Jefffrey. *Parents and Children: The Ethics of the Family.* Oxford University Press, 1982.

Brashier, Ralph C. *Inheritance Law and the Evolving Family.* Philadelphia: Temple University Press, 2004.

Bricker, Jesse, Lisa J. Dettling, Alice Henriques, Joanne W. Hsu, Kevin B. Moore, John Sabelhaus, Jeffrey Thompson, and Richard A. Windle. "Changes in U.S. Family Finances from 2010 to 2013: Evidence from the Survey of Consumer Finances." *Federal Reserve Bulletin* 100, 4 (September 2014).

Carter, Elizabeth R. "Tipping the Scales in Favor of Charitable Bequests: A Critique." *Pace Law Review* 34, 3 (2014).

Chester, Ronald. *Inheritance, Wealth, and Society.* Bloomington IN: Indiana University Press, 1982.

Clifford, Denis. *Plan Your Estate.* 13th Edition. Berkeley CA: Nolo, 2016.

Clignet, Remi P. "Ethnicity and inheritance." In *Inheritance and Wealth in America,* edited by Robert K. Miller Jr. and Stephen J. McNamee, 120-138. New York and London: Plenum Press, 1998.

Cunliffe, John, and Guido Erreygers, editors. *Inherited Wealth, Justice and Equality*. London and New York: Routledge, 2013.

Dunn, Thomas A., and John W. Phillips. "The timing and division of parental transfers to children." *Economics Letters* 54 (1997): 135-137.

Editors of the Encyclopaedia Britannica. "Napoleonic Code." *Encyclopaedia Britannica* (no date). https://www.britannica.com/topic/Napoleonic-Code.

Engels, Friedrich. *The Origin of the Family, Private Property and the State*. First published 1881. Translated by Tristram Hunt. Penguin Classics, 2010.

Erreygers, Guido, and Toon Vandevelde, editors. *Is Inheritance Legitimate? Ethical and Economic Aspects of Wealth Transfers*. New York: Springer, 1997.

Fellows, Mary Louise, Rita J. Simon, and William Rau. "Public attitudes about property distribution at death and intestate succession laws in the United States." *Law and Social Inquiry* 3, 2 (1978): 319-391.

Fisher, Roger, and William Ury, with Bruce Patton, editor. *Getting to Yes: Negotiating Agreement Without Giving In*. Penguin Books, 2011.

Fitz, Nicholas. "Economic Inequality: It's Far Worse Than You Think." *Scientific American*, March 31, 2015.

Gilligan, Carol. "Moral orientation and moral development." In *Women and Moral Theory*, edited by Eva Feder Kittay and Diana T. Meyers, 19-33. Totowa NJ: Rowman & Littlefield, 1987.

Glendon, Mary Ann, and Max Rheinstein. "Inheritance Law." *Encyclopaedia Britannica*, 2015. https://www.britannica.com/topic/inheritance-law.

Glendon, Mary Ann, and Max Rheinstein. 2015. "Intestate succession." *Encyclopaedia Britannica*, 2015. https://www.britannica.com/topic/inheritance-law/intestate/succession#ref83749.

Graetz, Michael J. and Ian Shapiro. *Death by a Thousand Cuts: The Fight over Taxing Inherited Wealth.* Princeton, NJ: Princeton University Press, 2005.

Gunderson, Joan R. "Women and Inheritance in America." In *Inheritance and Wealth in America*, edited by Robert K. Miller, Jr. and Stephen J. McNamee, 91-118. New York and London: Plenum Press, 1998.

Hall, Julie. *How to Divide Your Family's Estate and Heirlooms Peacefully & Sensibly.* Charlotte NC: The Estate Lady Publications, 2010.

Hertz, Frederick, Ralph Warner, and Toni Ihara. *Living Together: A Legal Guide for Unmarried Couples* (15th edition). Berkeley, CA: Nolo, 2013.

Hurme, Sally Balch. *ABA/AARP Checklist for My Family: A Guide to My History, Financial Plans and Final Wishes.* Chicago: ABA Publishing, 2015.

Jamoussi, Zouheir. *Primogeniture and Entail in England: A Survey of their History and Representation in Literature.* Cambridge: Cambridge Scholars Publishing, 2011.

Kim, Kyunmin, David J. Eggebeen, Steven H. Zarit, Kira S. Birditt, and Karen L. Fingerman. "Agreement between aging parent's bequest intention and middle-aged child's inheritance expectation." *Gerontologist*, 53, 6 (2013): 1020–1031.

Kittay, Eva Feder, and Diana T. Meyers, editors. *Women and Moral Theory*. Totowa NJ: Rowman & Littlefield, 1987.

Leslie, Melanie B. "The Myth of Testamentary Freedom," *Arizona Law Review* 38, 235 (1996).

Levinson, Kate. *Emotional Currency: A Woman's Guide to Building a Healthy Relationship with Money*. New York: Random House, 2011.

Light, Audrey, and Kathleen McGarry. *Why Parents Play Favorites: Explanations for Unequal Bequests*. NBER Working Paper No. 9745. Cambridge MA: National Bureau of Economic Research, 2003.

Maine, William Sumner Henry. *Ancient Law, Its Connection with the Early History of Society, and Its Relation to Modern Ideas*. London: Dent, 1965. First published 1861.

Malcolm, Janet. *Two Lives: Gertrude and Alice*. Yale University Press, 2008.

Marx, Karl, and Friedrich Engels. *Collected Works: Volume 41*. "Letters 1860-64". London: Lawrence and Wishart, 1985.

MetLife. *The MetLife Study of Inheritance and Wealth Transfer to Baby Boomers*. New York: MetLife Mature Market Institute, 2010.

Miller, Robert K. Jr., and Stephen J. McNamee, editors. *Inheritance and Wealth in America*. New York and London: Plenum Press, 1998.

Mnookin, Robert. *Bargaining with the Devil: When to Negotiate, When to Fight.* New York: Simon and Schuster, 2010.

National Academies of Sciences, Engineering, and Medicine. *The Growing Gap in Life Expectancy by Income: Implications for Federal Programs and Policy Responses.* Washington, DC: National Academies Press, 2015.

National Conference of Commissioners on Uniform State Laws. 2010. *Uniform Probate Code (1969) (Amended 2010).* www.uniformlaws.org.

Nussbaum, Martha C. *Political Emotions: Why Love Matters for Justice.* Belknap, 2015.

Pearson, Katherine C. "Filial support laws in the modern era: domestic and international comparison of enforcement practices for laws requiring adult children to support indigent parents." *Elder Law Journal* 269, 20 (2013): 1-31.

Pfeffer, Fabian R., and Robert F. Schoeni. "How Inequality Shapes Our Future." *The Russell Sage Foundation Journal of the Social Sciences,* 2, 1 (2016), 2-22

Piketty, Thomas, and Gabriel Zucman. "Wealth and inheritance in the long run." *Handbook of Income Distribution,* Volume 2B, 1303-1368. Elsevier, 2015. Piketty.pse.ens.fr/files/PikettyZucman2014HID.pdf.

Randolph, Mary. *The Executor's Guide: Settling a Loved One's Estate or Trust.* Berkeley, CA: Nolo, 2016.

Rawls, John. *Justice as Fairness: A Restatement.* Edited by Erin Kelly. Cambridge MA: Belknap Press, 2001.

Rosenfeld, Jeffrey P. "Will Contests." In *Inheritance and Wealth in America,* edited by Robert K. Miller Jr. and Stephen J. McNamee, 173-192. New York and London: Plenum Press, 1998.

Sackler, Lori R., with Toddi Gutner. *The M Word. The Money Talk Every Family Needs to Have About Wealth and Their Financial Future.* New York: McGraw Hill, 2013.

Saez, Emmanuel, and Gabriel Zucman. "Exploding wealth inequality in the United States." Washington Center for Equitable Growth, 2014.

Sen, Amartya. *The Idea of Justice.* Cambridge, MA: Belknap Press, 2009.

Shammas, Carole, Marylynn Salmon and Michel Dahlin. *Inheritance in America: From Colonial Times to the Present.* New Brunswick and London: Rutgers University Press, 1987.

Shammas, Carole. "Re-Assessing the Married Women's Property Acts." *Journal of Women's History* 6, 1 (1994): 9-30.

Sommers, Christina Hoff. "Filial Morality." In *Women and Moral Theory,* edited by Eva Feder Kittay and Diana T. Meyers, 69-94. Totowa NJ: Rowman & Littlefield, 1987.

Stum, Marlene S. "'I Just Want to Be Fair': Interpersonal Justice in Intergenerational Transfers of Non-Titled Property." *Family Relations* 48, 2 (1999): 159-166.

Stum, Marlene S. "Families and Inheritance Decisions: Examining Non-Titled Property Transfers." *Journal of Family and Economic Issues* 21, 2 (2000): 177-202.

Stum, Marlene S. "Financing Long-Term Care: Examining Decisions Outcomes and Systemic Influences from the Perspective of Family Members." *Journal of Family and Economic Issues* 22, 1 (2001): 25-53.

Sullivan, Paul. "A Wider Path to Dynastic Wealth." *New York Times*, November 12, 2016.

Sussman, Marvin B., Judith N. Cates, and David T. Smith. *The Family and Inheritance.* New York: Russell Sage Foundation, 1970.

Sweeney, Cynthia D'Aprix. *The Nest. A Novel.* New York: HarperCollins, 2016.

Tannen, Deborah. *You Just Don't Understand: Women and Men in Conversation.* Ballantine Books, 1991.

Taylor, Janet E., and Joan E. Norris. "Sibling Relationships, Fairness, and Conflict Over Transfer of the Farm." *Family Relations* 49, 3 (2000): 277-283.

UBS. "Begin before the end: Why families need to have inheritance conversations now." *UBS Investor Watch 3Q,* 2014.

United States Census Bureau. 2012. *Statistical Abstract of the United States: 2012.* www.census.gov/compendia/statab/2012/tables/12s0586.pdf.

United States Department of Health and Human Services, Administration on Aging. *A Profile of Older Americans: 2014.*

Velasquez, Manuel, Claire Andre, Thomas Shanks, S.J., and Michael J. Meyer. "Justice and Fairness." Markula Center for Applied Ethics, Santa Clara University, 2014.

Vornovitsky, Marina, Alfred Gottschalck and Adam Smith. "Distribution of Household Wealth in the U.S.: 2000 to 2011." United States Census Bureau, 2014. https://www.census.gov/people/wealth/files/wealth distribution 2000 to 2011.pdf.

Warren, Anne. "Choosing the Objects of Your Bounty: Estate Planning for Unmarried Individuals and Individuals Without Children." *Philanthropy & Wealth Planning* (Brown Brothers Harriman, December 5, 2016).

Wegge, Simone. "Inheritance Systems." In *Oxford Encyclopedia of Economic History*, edited by Joel Mokyr (Oxford University Press, 2003), 77-83.

Zagorsky, Jay L. "Do people save or spend their inheritances? Understanding what happens to inherited wealth." *Journal of Family and Economic Issues* 34, 1 (2013): 64-76.

www.ingramcontent.com/pod-product-compliance
Lightning Source LLC
Chambersburg PA
CBHW071425180526
45170CB00001B/225